Too Tough?

Paul
Borthwick

Jan
Johnson

David C. Cook Publishing Co.
Elgin, Illinois—Weston, Ontario

Custom Curriculum
Too Tough?

Published by David C. Cook Publishing Co.
850 North Grove Ave., Elgin, IL 60120
Cable address: DCCOOK
Series creator: John Duckworth
Series editor: Randy Southern
Editor: Anne Dinnan
Option writers: Stan Campbell, Nelson E. Copeland, Jr., and Ellen Larson
Designer: Bill Paetzold
Cover illustrator: Tim Lee
Inside illustrator: Al Hering
Printed in U.S.A.

ISBN: 0-7814-5007-1

CONTENTS

Sessions by Jan Johnson
Options by Stan Campbell, Nelson E. Copeland, Jr., and Ellen Larson

About the Authors

Jan Johnson is a California writer who has taught young people in church and at school, and has been active in cross-cultural ministry.

Stan Campbell has been a youth worker for over eighteen years, and has written several books on youth ministry including the *BibleLog* series (SonPower) and the *Quick Studies* series (David C. Cook). He and his wife, Pam, are youth directors at Lisle Bible Church in Lisle, Illinois.

Nelson E. Copeland, Jr. is a nationally known speaker and the author of several youth resources including *Great Games for City Kids* (Youth Specialties) and *A New Agenda for Urban Youth* (Winston-Derek). He is president of the Christian Education Coalition for African-American Leadership (CECAAL), an organization dedicated to reinforcing educational and cultural excellence among urban teenagers. He also serves as youth pastor at the First Baptist Church in Morton, Pennsylvania.

Ellen Larson is an educator and writer with degrees in education and theology. She has served as minister of Christian education in several churches, teaching teens and children, as well as their teachers. Her experience also includes teaching in public schools. She is the author of several books for Christian education teachers, and frequently leads training seminars for volunteer teachers. Ellen and her husband live in San Diego and are the parents of two daughters.

You've Made the Right Choice!

Thanks for choosing **Custom Curriculum**! We think your choice says at least three things about you:

(1) You know your group pretty well, and want your program to fit that group like a glove;

(2) You like having options instead of being boxed in by some far-off curriculum editor;

(3) You have a small mole on your left forearm, exactly two inches above the elbow.

OK, so we were wrong about the mole. But if you like having choices that help you tailor meetings to fit your kids, **Custom Curriculum** *is* the best place to be.

Going through Customs

In this (and every) **Custom Curriculum** volume, you'll find

• five great sessions you can use anytime, in any order.

• reproducible student handouts, at least one per session.

• a truckload of options for adapting the sessions to your group (more about that in a minute).

• a helpful get-you-ready article by a youth expert.

• clip art for making posters, fliers, and other kinds of publicity to get kids to your meetings.

Each **Custom Curriculum** session has three to six steps. No matter how many steps a session has, it's designed to achieve these goals:

• *Getting together.* Using an icebreaker activity, you'll help kids be glad they came to the meeting.

• *Getting thirsty.* Why should kids care about your topic? Why should they care what the Bible has to say about it? You'll want to take a few minutes to earn their interest before you start pouring the "living water."

• *Getting the Word.* By exploring and discussing carefully selected passages, you'll find out what God has to say.

• *Getting the point.* Here's where you'll help kids make the leap from principles to nitty-gritty situations they are likely to face.

• *Getting personal.* What should each group member do as a result of this session? You'll help each person find a specific "next-step" response that works for him or her.

Each session is written to last 45 to 60 minutes. But what if you have less time—or more? No problem! **Custom Curriculum** is all about … options!

What Are My Options?

Every **Custom Curriculum** session gives you fourteen kinds of options:

• *Extra Action*—for groups that learn better when they're physically moving (instead of just reading, writing, and discussing).

• *Combined Junior High/High School*—to use when you're mixing age levels, and an activity or case study would be too "young" or "old" for part of the group.

• *Small Group*—for adapting activities that would be tough with groups of fewer than eight kids.

• *Large Group*—to alter steps for groups of more than twenty kids.

• *Urban*—for fitting sessions to urban facilities and multiethnic (especially African-American) concerns.

• *Heard It All Before*—for fresh approaches that get past the defenses of kids who are jaded by years in church.

• *Little Bible Background*—to use when most of your kids are strangers to the Bible, or haven't made a Christian commitment.

• *Mostly Guys*—to focus on guys' interests and to substitute activities they might be more enthused about.

• *Mostly Girls*—to address girls' concerns and to substitute activities they might prefer.

• *Extra Fun*—for longer, more "rowdy" youth meetings where the emphasis is on fun.

• *Short Meeting Time*—tips for condensing the session to 30 minutes or so.

• *Fellowship & Worship*—for building deeper relationships or enabling kids to praise God together.

• *Media*—to spice up meetings with video, music, or other popular media.

• *Sixth Grade*—appearing only in junior high/middle school volumes, this option helps you change steps that sixth graders might find hard to understand or relate to.

• *Extra Challenge*—appearing only in high school volumes, this option lets you crank up the voltage for kids who are ready for more Scripture or more demanding personal application.

Each kind of option is offered twice in each session. So in this book, you get *almost 150* ways to tweak the meetings to fit your group!

Customizing a Session

All right, you may be thinking. *With all of these options flying around, how do I put a session together? I don't have a lot of time, you know.*

We know! That's why we've made **Custom Curriculum** as easy to follow as possible. Let's take a look at how you might prepare an actual meeting. You can do that in four easy steps:

(1) *Read the basic session plan.* Start by choosing one or more of the goals listed at the beginning of the session. You have three to pick from: a goal that emphasizes *knowledge*, one that stresses *understanding*, and one that emphasizes *action*. Choose one or more, depending on what *you* want to accomplish. Then read the basic plan to see what will work for you and what might not.

(2) *Choose your options.* You don't *have* to use any options at all; the

basic session plan would work well for many groups, and you may want to stick with it if you have absolutely no time to consider options. But if you want a more perfect fit, check out your choices.

As you read the basic session plan, you'll see small symbols in the margin. Each symbol stands for a different kind of option. When you see a symbol, it means that kind of option is offered for that step. Turn to the page noted by the symbol and you'll see that option explained.

Let's say you have a small group, mostly guys who get bored if they don't keep moving. You'll want to keep an eye out for three kinds of options: Small Group, Mostly Guys, and Extra Action. As you read the basic session, you might spot symbols that tell you there are Small Group options for Step 1 and Step 3—maybe a different way to play a game so that you don't need big teams, and a way to cover several Bible passages when just a few kids are looking them up. Then you see symbols telling you that there are Mostly Guys options for Step 2 and Step 4—perhaps a substitute activity that doesn't require too much self-disclosure, and a case study guys will relate to. Finally you see symbols indicating Extra Action options for Step 2 and Step 3—maybe an active way to get kids' opinions instead of handing out a survey, and a way to act out some verses instead of just looking them up.

After reading the options, you might decide to use four of them. You base your choices on your personal tastes and the traits of your group that you think are most important right now. **Custom Curriculum** offers you more options than you'll need, so you can pick your current favorites and plug others into future meetings if you like.

(3) *Use the checklist.* Once you've picked your options, keep track of them with the simple checklist that appears at the end of each option section (just before the start of the next session plan). This little form gives you a place to write down the materials you'll need too—since they depend on the options you've chosen.

(4) *Get your stuff together.* Gather your materials; photocopy any Repro Resources (reproducible student sheets) you've decided to use. And . . . you're ready!

The Custom Curriculum Challenge

Your kids are fortunate to have you as their leader. You see them not as a bunch of generic teenagers, but as real, live, unique kids. You care whether you really connect with them. That's why you're willing to take a few extra minutes to tailor your meetings to fit.

It's a challenge to work with real, live kids, isn't it? We think you deserve a standing ovation for taking that challenge. And we pray that **Custom Curriculum** helps you shape sessions that shape lives for Jesus Christ and His kingdom.

—The Editors

Talking to Kids about the Tough Teachings of Jesus

by Paul Borthwick

I was in the middle of a conversation with a friend when several large portions of my old Bible fell out of its cracked binding. My friend lunged to save them as they fell. Without thinking, I quipped, "That's all right. They were problem texts anyhow."

We laughed because we both knew of tough passages in Scripture which we would rather do without.

In preparing for messages or Bible studies, we've all probably come across very difficult passages (either tough ones to apply or difficult ones to understand), and thought to ourselves, *I really wish that Jesus hadn't said that.*

But if we truly believe that we should teach the "whole will of God" (Acts 20:27) and that "all Scripture is God-breathed" and is profitable for growth (II Timothy 3:16), then we cannot shrink away from the tough texts—whether they're addressing doctrinal issues or lifestyle convictions.

One thing we need to remember before we start is that following Jesus is difficult. We would all like an instant Christianity that's "as easy as 1-2-3" to understand, but this is not the life of faith. Following Jesus is described in the Bible with images of running a marathon or wrestling in a fight. Tackling tough issues and texts is simply part of the discipline of discipleship.

Foundation for Success

The best foundation to build upon as we start this series is honesty. We do not need to pretend that these are texts that we have mastered and that cause no problems for us. Instead, we should feel free to admit that these are difficult questions, and then illustrate that point with the questions we personally bring to the texts. For example:

• How can we flee from lust in an X-rated society in which almost every TV program, movie, or song seems laced with sexual innuendo?

• When I ask in faith for something, why doesn't Jesus respond as He promised?

• How can I keep from worrying when life seems out of control?

• Does following Jesus really mean loving enemies who have hurt me deeply, rejected me, or belittled me?

• What if I enjoy the thought of being rich? Does this disqualify me from being a Christian?

I once thought that working with young people meant protecting them from these tough texts and difficult issues. I suppose I thought, *My job is to get them grounded in the faith; later in life they can think about these things.*

But as we studied the Bible together, the tough issues were too prevalent to be avoided. If I tried to dodge the issues, group members knew that I was being selective in what Scripture I applied to our lives. I came to the conclusion that integrity demanded that I address these tough texts. No matter what their ages, the young people in our groups need to know that following Jesus is a rigorous challenge.

Proceed with Caution

As we teach these tough texts, there are two pitfalls to avoid. First, we need to be careful not to ridicule other people's interpretations of these texts. We can explain our differences with others in the Christian tradition without belittling those who adhere to other views.

For example, in trying to understand the extreme and literal application of the passage about "selling all and giving it to the poor," I made some jokes about what I thought was the weird lifestyle of those who had taken vows of poverty for Jesus. For the young people in our ministry who were from Roman Catholic families, this seemed like an unnecessary criticism of some heavily committed people, and my ill-timed humor caused me to lose credibility as a teacher.

The same loss of credibility may occur if we mock the faith healers who have different interpretations of the text about "Ask, and it will be done for you" or the believers who understand "Love your enemies" as a command for total pacifism.

Remember, our goal is to help group members understand the texts as they affect their lives—not to excuse ourselves from grappling with the texts by ridiculing those who we think may have misapplied or overapplied them.

Second, we need to be careful not to talk *at* group members. Instead, we should talk *with* them. This reflects the basic foundation of honesty. When we engage in the study of texts that we do not understand, some of us have a tendency to resort to impersonal lecturing.

We report on the various ways that the church has understood these texts in the past. We get our explanations out of commentaries, and in so doing, we communicate to group members that we are seeking to understand the texts intellectually without really caring about what it means in our lives.

If we're unclear or insecure about the meaning of these texts, no scholarly lecture or commentary quotations will hide this from our group members. Instead, they will see us as being afraid to deal with the real meaning of the texts. It's far better to let group members know that we are fellow learners with them, striving to understand what these hard teachings of Jesus say to us today.

Building for Effectiveness

To effectively address the tough teachings of Jesus covered in this book, you'll need to emphasize and/or demonstrate three principles: grace, mercy, and empathy.

(1) Grace. In a discussion in our group about selling everything and giving to the poor, we began talking about some of our church-supported missionaries who, in the eyes of our group members, were

the most vivid illustration of this passage.

One group member asked about Dr. Bob, a missionary doctor who had left what was obviously a lucrative practice to go work in central Africa. As the group members talked, I realized that they were under the impression that Bob had made this "once and for all" decision without a struggle, and that he never thought about returning to the United States to increase his earning power.

I knew something of the struggles that missionaries like Bob went through, so I explained to the group members that obeying the command was not a "once and for all" issue but rather a lifetime process. Did Bob ever struggle with that decision? Indeed! Had he thought about a return to the States? Often!

In teaching that text, I realized that it was my job to emphasize the grace of God in obeying His commands. I needed to remind group members that Jesus will give us grace to obey these commands. In a time when group members were feeling that the Christian life was far out of their reach, I pointed them to the fact of God's grace—where He commands, He also will empower to fulfill.

(2) Mercy. When you tackle the the tough teachings ahead of you in this book, you'll discover that many group members have already failed. Lustful thoughts may already be a daily occurrence. Worrying? Some will have already established life patterns built on anxiety and stress. Love your enemies? For some group members, hate has anchored itself deep in their souls.

As a result, we need to emphasize mercy. Our teaching of these tough commands should be intertwined with what one person calls the "Gospel of the second chance." Group members can respond to these texts more effectively if they understand forgiveness and the freedom we have as Christians to get back up after we fail.

Haddon Robinson's essay entitled "A Little Verse for Losers" helped me emphasize this mercy with group members. In this essay, Robinson recalls the story of Jonah, who responded to a hard command of God by going the opposite direction from God's command.

With an emphasis on mercy, Robinson points the reader to Jonah 3:1: "And the word of the Lord came to Jonah a second time." This "verse for losers" reminds us that God, in His great love, did not give up on Jonah—and He will not give up on us. This is a truth we all need to hear in the context of these tough commands.

(3) Empathy. When I embark on the study of texts like these, I do better if I think of myself as a "fellow struggler" rather than the teacher. With the "fellow struggler" perspective, I am free to share out of my own life.

I learned this lesson from an 84-year-old Christian leader who was leading a men's seminar at our church one summer day. As a young Christian, I was wrestling with the meaning of Jesus' teaching in the Sermon on the Mount about lustful thoughts and adultery in the mind. I could not seem to succeed in obeying this text.

The aged veteran started the seminar. In response to some of the scanty summer attire of women around the church, he prayed, "Lord, deliver me from lustful thoughts." At that moment, I realized, *I can listen to this guy; he knows what I'm going through.* He presented himself as a fellow struggler rather than an accomplished veteran.

So empathize. When the study covers "Sell all and give to the poor," pray honestly before group members, "Lord, You know that I am coming to this passage with the desire to rationalize it away. Help me to hear Your voice." Admit the struggle with anxiety. Confess the difficulty in loving enemies.

Such empathy allows group members to see us as real people who are genuinely battling with the application of these tough texts.

Into the Fight

In the weeks ahead, this study will take you into texts that you might rather tear out of your Bible and throw away. Instead of taking the easy route, accept the challenge of teaching these tough sayings of Jesus. It may not be easy—but neither is following Jesus.

Paul Borthwick is minister of missions at Grace Chapel in Lexington, Massachusetts. A former youth pastor and frequent speaker to youth workers, he is the author of several books, including Organizing Your Youth Ministry *and* Feeding Your Forgotten Soul: Spiritual Growth for Youth Workers *(Zondervan).*

The images on these two pages are designed to help you promote this course within your church and community. Feel free to photocopy anything here and adapt it to fit your publicity needs. The stuff on this page could be used as a flier that you send or hand out to kids—or as a bulletin insert. The stuff on the next page could be used to add visual interest to newsletters, calendars, bulletin boards, or other promotions. Be creative and have fun!

What's the Toughest Thing Jesus Said?

Of all the hard sayings of Jesus, which one do you find most difficult?

   a. Don't look at anyone lustfully.

   b. You can have enough faith to move mountains.

   c. Don't worry about anything.

   d. Love your enemies.

   e. Sell everything you have and give it to the poor.

   f. All of the above!

For the next few weeks, we'll be tackling some of Jesus' toughest teachings in a new course called *Too Tough?* It won't be easy, but it'll be worth it!

Who:

When:

Where:

Questions? Call:

Too Tough?

Too Tough?

Have you heard the latest?

Use your head.

Have a heart.

Was Jesus joking?

Take courage.

15

Are Sexual Thoughts Always Sinful?

YOUR GOALS FOR THIS SESSION:

Choose one or more

☐ To help kids distinguish between lust and normal sexual thoughts.

☐ To help kids understand that the Bible condemns lust, but it doesn't condemn sex or sexual thoughts.

☐ To help kids choose behaviors that will lead them away from lust to purity and respect of others.

☐ Other _____

Your Bible Base:

II Samuel 11:1-5
Matthew 5:27-30
1 Thessalonians 4:7
Hebrews 4:15, 16

The Great Cover-Up

(Needed: Several rolls of elastic bandage)

Divide group members into two teams. Give each team several elastic bandages—the kind you would use for wrapping a sprained ankle. Before explaining the game, ask each team to choose a volunteer.

Then give the following instructions: **When I say go, start winding the bandage around your volunteer, covering him or her up as much as possible. Go!**

While kids are wrapping their team members, call out expert advice on how to do the job (over, under, around, through the legs, and so on). When one team has finished, evaluate the cover-up job. If the other team isn't too far behind, allow it to finish. Then judge between the two teams.

Announce which team pulled off the best cover-up, applaud the winning team, and let your volunteers unwrap themselves.

Then say: **Ever since Adam and Eve sewed together the fig leaves, people have covered themselves up in varying stages, hoping to prevent sexual temptation. Unfortunately, covering up temptation doesn't make it go away.**

The Fine Line of Lust

(Needed: Index cards prepared according to instructions, tape, chalkboard and chalk or newsprint and marker)

Before this session, write the following items on separate index cards:
- Ads
- Music videos
- Cable stations
- Romance novels
- Magazines like *Playboy* and *Playgirl*

- R-rated movies
- NC-17 movies
- Adult movies
- Thong bathing suits
- Topless sunbathing
- Trashy TV movies
- Swimsuit issue of *Sports Illustrated*
- Hunk-a-month calendars

Depending on the maturity of your group members, you may want to separate guys and girls into two groups for better discussion. Some kids might feel more comfortable talking about these issues in this "safer" atmosphere.

[NOTE: Kids might ask you about other sexual matters that concern them: masturbation, wet dreams, and so on. If so, you'll need to decide whether or not to sidetrack this discussion of Jesus' tough teaching on lust and tackle these other issues.]

Say: **Although God created us with sexual desires, He placed restrictions on how we express those desires. So what's the deal? How do we know what's right or what's wrong?**

Hand out the index cards to various kids. You'll also need a roll of tape on hand. Draw a line down the middle of the board. Point to one side of the line and say: **Anything we put on this side of the line is OK. We don't have any problems with this stuff. But when we cross the line** (drag your finger across the line on the board)**, the stuff on this side is wrong and makes us uncomfortable.**

One at a time, ask each group member to read aloud his or her card. As a group, decide on which side of the line each item belongs. Encourage group members to explain their reasons for why one thing is OK and another thing isn't. If group members can't agree on something, ask them to vote on it, and go with the majority decision. No matter how much you may disagree with a decision, let it stand. When a decision has been reached, the group member with the card will tape it to the appropriate side of the board.

Choose one of the items group members put on the "OK" side of the line and ask: **Is there any way this item might cross the line and become wrong?** (Yes. For example, some romance novels are "soft porn" in disguise. Or a guy might start obsessing about the models in a *Sports Illustrated* swimsuit edition, which might lead to unhealthy fantasies and unfulfilled desires.)

Explain: **There's a fine line between positive sexual desires and negative desires. But how do you know when you've crossed that line? While on earth, Jesus talked about that line; but instead of making things easier, He seemed to make them more difficult to understand.**

OPTIONS

LARGE GROUP

HEARD IT ALL BEFORE

MOSTLY GUYS

EXTRA FUN

MEDIA

SHORT MEETING TIME

URBAN

STEP 3

What's Love Got to Do with It?

(Needed: Bibles, chalkboard and chalk or newsprint and marker)

OPTIONS

SMALL GROUP

HEARD IT ALL BEFORE

LITTLE BIBLE BACKGROUND

FELLOWSHIP & WORSHIP

MOSTLY GIRLS

JR. HIGH HIGH SCHOOL COMBINED

EXTRA CHALLENGE

Say: **A lot of Jesus' teachings are tough to understand and even tougher to practice—like the one we're going to talk about in Matthew 5:27-30.** Have group members turn to the passage in their Bibles. Ask a volunteer to read it aloud.

Then say: **Look at verse 28 again: "Anyone who looks at a woman lustfully has already committed adultery with her in his heart." And the same thing goes for a woman looking lustfully at a man.**

What's your first reaction to this teaching? (It's unrealistic; it's unreasonable; it's too rigid.)

You might want to explain what Jesus was doing in His Sermon on the Mount. Because of the hypocrisy of the Pharisees, Jesus set a higher standard for His followers and elevated the Ten Commandments. Not only was murder wrong, but so was getting angry with someone. Not only was adultery wrong, but so were lustful thoughts. The Pharisees obeyed the law externally, but it was all a sham because they broke the commands internally.

What makes this teaching tough? (It seems impossible to keep! You could drive yourself crazy trying to figure out what is or isn't a lustful thought. Besides, what does the word "lust" mean anyhow?)

Before we go any further, let's define our terms. Lust is usually forbidden or unchecked sexual desire. It's a craving or intense desire or need. It doesn't necessarily have anything to do with love.

Let's look at David's example. He was the greatest king Israel ever had, an ancestor of Jesus, and a man after God's own heart. But he had a problem with lust. Turn back in your Bibles to II Samuel 11:1-5 and look at the opening scene of this made-for-TV story.

Give group members a chance to read the passage. Then ask:
Where did David go wrong? (He gave in to sexual temptation. He let his sexual desires get out of hand and went after Bathsheba.)

David was also in the wrong place at the wrong time. According to verse one, King David probably should have been off to war as expected instead of hanging around the palace.

What could David have done to prevent his temptation

from becoming lust and eventually becoming sin? Use the following ideas to supplement group members' responses.

• *Pray about the temptation.* David, the author of many moving prayers and psalms, should have prayed when he saw Bathsheba. Then he should have left the temptation zone.

• *Become accountable to someone you trust.* David probably had many advisors he trusted. He could have gone to one of them to talk about his temptation.

• *Get a wife.* This isn't a solution to lust. Some people think that being married solves lust problems, but it doesn't. According to II Samuel 3:2-5, David had at least six wives. Yet he still gave in to his lust.

Ask: **Why doesn't being married solve the problem of lust?** (Even if you're married, you can be attracted to others. They may seem more attractive, more tender, more fun than your spouse.)

• *Get a life.*

Ask: **Before David was king, he was a skillful warrior. What was he doing in this passage?** (*Not* going to war with his troops [see II Samuel 11:1]. Some people think that David gave in to his sexual temptation because he was bored. He wasn't doing what he was supposed to do—to lead the battle.)

Ask: **Do you think it was wrong for David to feel tempted?** After several group members have expressed their opinions, have them turn to Hebrews 4:15, 16. Ask a volunteer to read the verses aloud.

Then say: **Can you see the difference between the temptation to sin and sin itself? It wasn't wrong for David to feel the sexual pressures, but it was wrong for him to give in to the pressure and sin. At some point he crossed the line between temptation and sin, fueled by his lust.**

Have group members form teams of three or four. Instruct each team to compare the story of David and Bathsheba and the Hebrews 4:15, 16 passage with the tough teaching of Jesus in Matthew 5:28.

Say: **As a team, come up with a one- or two-sentence summary of Jesus' command in Matthew 5:28**. (For example: Anyone who looks at someone and is consumed with thoughts of having sex with that person has already committed adultery. The temptation isn't wrong, but thinking about it all of the time, making plans to do it, giving in to it, and committing a sin is wrong.)

When teams have finished, have them read their summaries. You'll probably hear some recurring themes such as being consumed with sex, giving in to the desire, or feeding a lustful thought until it becomes an act.

Summarize: **A sexual thought comes and goes, but a craving grows and consumes you. And just as adultery wrecks a marriage, lust destroys relationships because you're treating people as objects or a collection of body parts.**

Handled well, sex can be a wonderful part of a lifelong

commitment in marriage. Handled badly, it can lead to a lifetime of loneliness, frustration, and guilt.

Lustbusters

(Needed: Copies of Repro Resource 1, pencils, Bibles, poster board prepared according to instructions, marker)

Before the session, you'll need to draw four continuums (i.e., horizontal or vertical bars) on a piece of poster board. At the left end of each continuum, write, "OK Zone"; in the middle write, "Warning Zone"; and at the right end, write, "Danger Zone."

Distribute copies of "Lustbusters" (Repro Resource 1) and pencils. Give group members a few minutes to read through the situations.

Explain: **For each situation, you'll need to decide whether the person is in the "OK Zone," and doesn't have a problem with lust; whether the person's in the "Warning Zone," and is headed for trouble; or whether the person is in the "Danger Zone," and has big problems with lust.**

When everyone is finished, hold up the poster board with the continuums on it. Say: **I'm going to start shading in this first bar for Denise. Yell for me to stop when you think I've reached the right zone for her.** Do this for each character on Repro Resource 1.

Each time someone shouts stop, stop; then ask if everyone agrees or whether should you keep going. When the majority of your group members tell you to stop, do so and ask them why the person belongs in that particular zone.

Have group members form teams of two or three to complete the bottom section of Repro Resource 1. Encourage them to list as many specific actions as they can think of that lead to and away from lust. Use the following suggestions to supplement group members' ideas.

Things that may lead to lust
- Thinking of people just as bodies
- Looking at and reading pornography
- Daydreaming about having sex with certain people
- Watching a lot of TV
- Being obsessive about looks and outward appearance
- Thinking of sex as a way to gain acceptance or someone's love

Things that may lead away from lust
• Being interested and active in all kinds of activities
• Handling feelings in positive ways such as journal writing or talking to people you trust
• Having some sort of valuable focus or goal for your life
• Developing healthy relationships with all kinds of people
When the teams are finished, have each one share and explain its list.

STEP
5

You Can Do It

Say: **Regardless of what you see in the movies or on TV or hear in pop music, you can—with God's help—resist sexual temptation.**

Ask group members to pair up with a friend of the same sex. Instruct them to tell their partners about a time they successfully resisted sexual temptation. You might ask the following questions to get them started.

• **Have you ever walked away from a display of sexually explicit magazines?**

• **Have you ever refused to respond to someone's sexual advances?**

• **Have you ever played basketball or done something else when you started to fantasize sexually?**

• **Have you ever decided not to hang out with a certain person who talks about sex a lot?**

After a few minutes, call the group back together. Read aloud I Thessalonians 4:7: "For God did not call us to be impure, but to live a holy life."

Explain: **Because God called us to be pure, He will help us overcome sexual temptation and sin.**

Close the session in prayer, thanking God for creating sex and asking Him to help your group members handle their sexuality in appropriate ways. Invite anyone who needs to talk with you privately after the session to do so.

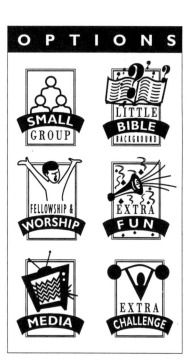

Lustbusters

D E N I S E likes to hang out at the pool in the summer—mostly to look at guys, flirt a little, and get lots of sun. Denise likes to "rate" guys and make comments about their looks. She and her friends make sure they look super-good in their suits, so they diet and do whatever else it takes to look good.

S T E V E doesn't have a life, except for cable TV. He likes to watch the adult channels on weekends. He also has a stash of *Playboy* magazines that he looks at a lot. Steve wonders why he has so much trouble talking with girls. After all, he thinks about them all the time—well, actually, he thinks about their *bodies* all the time.

K A R E N ' S parents are in the process of a divorce, and she feels lonely and rejected. If she had a boyfriend, she'd probably do anything to hang on to him. Fortunately, she's making a lot of friends in youth group and at school. She also spends a lot of time with a couple from church who are youth sponsors.

C R A I G is always on the go. He plays basketball and runs track. His next-door neighbor is showing him how to repair cars. Craig has a girlfriend, but they don't seem to have the problems resisting sex that other couples do. It does bug him when his friends keep asking when he and his girlfriend are going to "do it," but Craig hasn't given in to the pressure.

THINGS THAT MAY LEAD TO LUST	THINGS THAT MAY LEAD AWAY FROM LUST
_____	_____
_____	_____
_____	_____
_____	_____
_____	_____
_____	_____
_____	_____

Step 1

A particularly active group may be too antsy to stand by and watch as other team members do the bandage-wrapping activity. Another option in such cases is to let the group split into two-person teams. Provide each pair with a roll of toilet paper and instructions for one person to wrap the other as completely as possible. To keep anyone from taking too much time, you might want to establish a time limit at the beginning. When everyone is finished, let anyone "model" who wishes to do so. Then determine which team(s) did the best job. (You may also want to have a camera on hand. Usually the ones who get wrapped up don't have much of an opportunity to see the others clearly.)

Step 4

With a bit of modification, the scenarios on Repro Resource 1 can be made into skits. Divide into teams and let each team bring Denise, Steve, Karen, and Craig to life. Team members can act as friends, parents, or other people in the lives of the central character. As kids act out the scenes, they are likely to add revealing comments or actions that reflect similar situations they or their friends have experienced in real life. When they finish, you can make the same applications by determining whether each person is in the "OK Zone," "Warning Zone," or "Danger Zone." But in this case, based on how the characters were portrayed in the skits, group members might also be able to make specific recommendations as to what the characters could do differently to stay in the "OK Zone."

Step 3

As you discuss Matthew 5:27-30, assign a "body part" (eye, hand, foot, ear, etc.) to each group member. Then ask questions about lust—nothing embarrassing or too personal, but specific enough to require honest responses. For example:
Eyes—**Have you seen any TV shows or movies this week that focused on the sexual aspects of one of the characters? Have you looked at any magazines or catalogs that featured scantily clothed people as an attempt to turn you on or sell you something?**
Hands—**Have you picked up** *Playboy* **or a similar magazine this week? Did you pop a video that you knew contained nudity in your VCR?**
Feet—**Did you go to any R-rated movies this week? Did you go to any parties in which a lot of sexual activity was taking place?**
Ears—**Did you listen to any jokes that demeaned the opposite sex? Did you listen in on any 1-900 phone lines?**

Each time someone admits to involvement in one of these activities, "cut" him or her off from the rest of the body. After you "lose" several members, ask: **Could you blame your problem on some other body part?** Point out that if we go somewhere we don't belong, we usually end up seeing what we shouldn't see, doing what we shouldn't do, and hearing what we shouldn't hear.) Ask: **Which is worse: eliminating a problem area or letting it keep getting the rest of the body in trouble?** (The best option is to keep the body part, but eliminate its lustful activities.)

Step 5

Have kids answer the questions as a group rather than in pairs. Kids may be uncomfortable discussing lust in a group; but it's important for them to begin to open up to each other. Point out that if they can't even *discuss* the topic, they won't be able to effectively *help* each other.

Step 1

After the opening exercise, emphasize the importance of the subject you're about to discuss. Use the most recent statistics you can find about sexual activity and attitudes, but customize it for your group. Suppose you have twenty-five guys and twenty-five girls. Rather than explaining that surveys show that 54 % of high schoolers have had sex, you might say: **If this were an average group, 27 of you have already had sex. If you were all seniors, 36 of you** (72%) **would be sexually active. Two of you** (4%) **would have a sexually transmitted disease.** Statistics seem to change every day, so look for current ones. The previous statistics are from a study released in January, 1992, by the Centers for Disease Control. Here are some additional observations collected from 19,958 readers of *Sassy* magazine (October 1992):
• 67% of girls have told a guy "I love you" without meaning it. (Only 15% of guys said they had done the same to girls.)
• 62% of guys have stereotyped a girl as a slut because of the way she dressed.
• 91% of guys said it wouldn't bother them if a girl they liked thought they were virgins.
• 63% of guys and 68% of girls have turned down offers of sex with someone they liked.

Step 2

Rather than filling out index cards with the activities listed in the text, get group members involved in the process. Have each person give you a reason why some people *might* be led to lust. Explain that you're just looking for general problem areas, not personal ones. You might even want to make an elimination activity out of this. When someone is unable to come up with a new idea, he or she is out. Continue until you have just a few people left. Then jokingly applaud them for being the ones in your group who know the most about lust. Write the suggestions on index cards as they are named. Then discuss on which side of the line each one should go.

Step 2
Announce that you've discovered a device that cures people of lust. Then hand out blindfolds (or sunglasses with the lenses covered with dark paper). Have kids put them on. Ask: **How effective do you think this device will be in fighting lust? Why?** As a group, develop a list of situations in which people should consider wearing these devices. Examples might include looking at magazine racks, watching cable TV, walking past adult videos at the video store, etc. Ask: **If a device were developed that really stopped lust, how well do you think it would sell? Why? Who do you think would buy it? Who do you think would protest it?** Questions like these might get kids thinking about the subject in new ways. They might see that some people don't want to get rid of lust because they enjoy it too much.

Step 3
The story of David and Bathsheba is used a lot to deal with the topic of lust—as it should be. But if your group members don't seem to think they have anything else to learn, let them recreate the story in a variety of ways. One group might try to bring the story into a twentieth-century setting. Another might attempt to tell the story from a gender-reversal point of view. (Don't girls lust too?) It's one thing to *know* the facts of this story, but it may take a bit of creative writing to get your kids past the facts to deal with the mind-sets and emotions of the characters involved.

Step 3
Matthew 5:27-30 is a difficult passage for trained theologians to deal with—much less students without much Bible background. Before you even begin to deal with it, let group members do an impromptu skit. One person should play the CEO of a large company. Other people, two at a time, should come into the CEO's office. One person in each pair should accuse the other of a serious offense—and have the proof to back up his or her accusations. In the first pair, perhaps the offender has been embezzling money from the company. Another person might have gotten the company into serious tax trouble. Another could be running his own business using the CEO's company's resources (copier, paper, supplies, stamps, etc.). Have the CEO decide in each case what should happen to the offending employee. (Firing? Arrest? Both?) Then shift to the passage in Matthew and discuss how people are even more important than companies, so Jesus wants us to do whatever it takes to keep us from harming ourselves and/or others.

Step 5
As a summary of everything you've discussed, you might need to replace the discussion of personal resistance of temptation with one centered on exactly why lust (or even sexual activity) is such a big deal. If your kids are more attuned to secular culture than biblical truth, some of them may not have ever been taught that lust and premarital sex are wrong. Be sensitive to this possibility. If you suspect some of your group members need a bit more grounding before they can get serious about making personal commitments in resisting sexual temptation, close with a question-and-answer period. Be ready with some basic Bible texts that will help kids work through their questions (Galatians 5:19-23; Ephesians 5:1-14; Philippians 4:8, 9; I Thessalonians 4:1-12; etc.).

Step 3
One reason lust is such a potentially dangerous sin is that people don't usually like to talk about their sexual feelings—or even admit them to themselves. As you discuss lust openly in your group, try to plan ahead for the future when your kids aren't *in* the group. Have kids form teams of three with the people (of the same sex) in the group they know best. Ask them to commit to becoming "lust-escape partners." Explain that any time someone is feeling particularly vulnerable to lustful thoughts, he or she should be able to call one or both of his or her partners. If possible, the partners should try to do something together (jogging, shopping, etc.). If not, they can at least talk for a while until the person is able to "change the channel" of the thoughts going through his or her head. Partners might even pray for each other during these times—and on a regular basis. Explain that it may seem strange at first to call someone up and say, "I'm feeling a bit lustful right now. Would you like to talk?" But this is a better option than acting on one's lustful thoughts. Many people choose to call 1-900 numbers. Challenge your kids to call a friend instead.

Step 5
It's sometimes difficult to discuss sexual issues with teenagers without making sex sound horrible or evil. You might consider ending the discussion of lust with a "Celebration of Sex" ceremony. Challenge kids to think of all the reasons they can be thankful for sex at this point in their lives. (The reason they're here today is because their parents had sex; it's a wonderful gift of God that they can look forward to when they get married; etc.) Also have them express thanks for acceptable sexual activities during adolescence (hand holding, good-night kisses, talking with a date in a romantic setting, etc.). Do everything you can to affirm the good and right things about sex (in the proper context) even as you agree to take a hard stand against lust and improper sexual activity.

Step 3

As you discuss Matthew 5:28, before talking about David, ask your group members to define the word *lust*. Ask: **Is lust the same thing as having sexual desires? What about sexual thoughts? Why or why not?**

Step 4

After the continuums are marked for the situations on "Lustbusters" (Repro Resource 1), refer back to the character of Steve. Ask your girls whether they think they have a responsibility toward guys like Steve. Ask: **If Steve were a part of our group, what might you do to help him? Should you just avoid him until he changes his ways? Why or why not?** As a group, discuss girls' influence on and responsibility toward guys. Ask: **What do you think about girls' dressing in ways that make them feel good because of the attention they might receive from the guys? Is it just the guys' problem if the style of dress influences their thoughts?**

Step 1

Bring in some bath towels and soap. Say: **I thought we might need these later on. Can anyone guess why?** If no one guesses, explain that you're going to be talking about sex, and you thought group members might need to take cold showers after the session. Point out that you're going to talk specifically about lust. It shouldn't be hard to get guys talking about the subject, especially if there aren't any girls around. Ask: **How often do you think most guys think about sex? Why? What percent of the average guy's sexual thoughts would you say are "lustful"? How old were you when you had your first intense sexual thoughts? How did you feel at the time? Why do you think God gave us such strong sexual desires?**

Step 2

A favorite justification among many guys for their lusting is that they wouldn't lust if girls dressed more modestly. So while you have a group of guys together, discuss this. Ask: **To what extent are girls responsible for the things you think about them?** Moderate the discussion to encourage a lot of different opinions, but don't comment immediately on statements that are made. After a while, when you're ready to move on, ask: **What can you do to keep certain girls from dressing the way they do?** (Nothing.) **Where can you live so that you won't see girls dress in provocative ways?** (Not many places.) **So is it OK for you to go right on lusting as long as there are girls who choose to wear short skirts or thong bathing suits?** (Obviously not.) Help your guys see that while they're seldom, if ever, responsible for how other people dress, they are *always* responsible for how they relate to other people. Consequently, we *never* have the right to blame others for our lust problems. The only reason we look and lust is because we choose to. And the only way to prevent it is to choose not to look.

Step 2

Traditionally, guys are more outspoken about issues of lust and in admitting their involvement in lustful thoughts and expressions. It can be argued that the problem is just as prevalent among girls, but that they usually remain less open about it. Since girls probably receive more stares and comments than guys do, at least at this stage in life, give them an opportunity to turn the tables. Have the guys compete in a beauty contest. One option is to make it a "blind" contest in which the guys roll up their pants legs and hold their bare legs out from under a partition or blanket. No one should be able to tell whose leg is whose. Girls can then vote for #3, #7, or whomever. You should monitor the contest, and make sure this remains a fun activity for everyone. Afterward, discuss how the guys liked being the targets of attention based entirely on their physical attributes rather than intelligence, personality, or other positive features. Also point out how, if we aren't careful, teasing and "just for fun" comments can get out of hand, leading to hurt feelings, damaged self-image, lust, and other harmful results.

Step 5

Explain (tongue in cheek) that sometimes we don't begin to deal with lust quickly enough because we don't recognize it. Explain that you want all of your group members to show the others what a lustful expression looks like. They should use facial expressions only—no other body language. Perhaps you might go around the room, one at a time, and let kids try to appear lustful. Or you might have group members sit in a circle and simultaneously make their lustful faces. Have some fun with this. But then make a serious point that while you're having fun and laughing hard, it's hard to act genuinely lustful. That's an important thing to remember the next time you need to break out of a lustful mood. Stop thinking so much in sexual terms and go have some *real* fun with someone.

Step 2

As you consider sources of potential lust, turn on a television set and begin to flip through the channels (or watch some video clips you've recorded earlier). Have kids try to identify anything that might be intended to arouse sexual thoughts. Listen for sexual jokes, comments, double entendres, etc. Evaluate the dress and body language of the characters. Examine the relationships of the characters. Even if you don't find any terribly offensive examples while doing this, you are likely to at least jar the memories of your group. Ask: **What are some things you've seen on TV lately that you're glad we didn't see as a group right now?** Challenge group members to think of music videos, cable shows, dating shows, 900-number ads, and so forth.) **Do you think you build up an immunity to these kinds of things, or do you think that over time they are likely to have a bigger influence on you than you might think?**

Step 5

By now, you've discussed that certain magazines are common sources of lustful thoughts. Some people use the print media to make a lot of money by having millions of people lust over naked (or near-naked) models. So spend some time before you close thinking about how you might be able to *discourage* people from lusting. Create your own magazine to do this. Give it a title, decide on some key articles for the first issue, design a cover if you wish, and determine what regular columns and features it would need. (If your group is a bit more "spotlight oriented," let them do a pilot for a new TV show that would serve the same purpose. It should be good enough to be on against *Studs* and *Love Connection* and still hold viewers' attention.)

Step 1

One way to condense the session is to focus on the personal application. Most young people don't need a lot of convincing that lust is a problem they must deal with. One shortcut is to do the activity in Step 1 and then skip Step 2. When you get to Step 3, start by reading Matthew 5:27-30 followed immediately by II Samuel 11:1-5. Before discussing anything else, ask: **How could David have followed Jesus' instructions to "gouge out" an eye that offended him?** Let kids come to the conclusion that, rather than actually poking out his eye, David could simply have turned around and walked the other way. It would have been that easy. But he gave in to his lustful thoughts and his life was never the same. Then move on to Steps 4 and 5, trying to help kids see how *they* can "turn around" rather than give in to their own lustful thoughts.

Step 2

Perhaps you prefer to focus more on the Bible study aspects than the personal applications. If so, begin the session with Step 2. Then go through Step 3 as written. Be sure everyone understands the various Bible texts: Matthew 5:27-30; II Samuel 11:1-5; and Hebrews 4:15, 16. Step 4 can be eliminated. But if you do have time, brainstorm suggestions for the bottom of Repro Resource 1—things that may lead to lust and things that may lead away from lust. This can easily be used as a transition between Step 3 and Step 5.

Step 2

Tape a ten-foot line on the floor. Have all of your group members stand side by side on one side of the line. Then choose a volunteer to stand on the other side of the line. The object of the activity is for the volunteer to see how many times he or she can step over the line and back without being pulled over completely by the rest of the group. Each time the person jumps over the line and back, he or she gets a point. (To get a point, the person must have both feet on the other side of the line before he or she jumps back.) The rest of the group members must try to prevent the person from jumping back over the line. However, they may not reach across the line to grab him or her. Set a one-minute time limit. Then ask for other volunteers to try it. You might want to award a small prize to the person with the most points. Use the activity to introduce a discussion of how "crossing the line" with lust can be dangerous.

Step 4

If you have an advanced, mature group of kids, you might want to use the following situation in conjunction with Repro Resource 1: **James is a fifteen-year-old church youth who says he does not have a lust problem. But he frequently buys *Hustler* and *Playboy* to assist him when he masturbates. One of his friends knows what he does and has tried to confront him, but James's response is, "There's nothing wrong with this. After all, it's safer than sex and better than getting AIDS. I'm not hurting anybody."**

Step 3

It can be difficult to deal with junior highers when you get into sexual issues. You know that some of them are already dealing with issues like lust and other sexual temptations, but others may still be enjoying some degree of innocence that you don't want to shatter. So when it comes to forming discussion teams, try to group your kids according to experience. Try to keep the younger ones together while those you know are dealing with sexual issues talk among themselves. This kind of grouping should also help kids feel more comfortable. (The last thing you want is for one of your kids to feel inferior because he or she is in a group in which everyone else seems to be more sexually aware—which he or she might interpret as "experienced"—than he or she is.)

Step 4

To help target temptations that are particularly hard for younger teens to overcome, do a skit. You (or one of your group members) should assume the role of an unscrupulous advertising executive. Your client manufactures condoms geared especially for high school students. As a ruthless ad person, your idea is to do whatever it takes to get junior highers sexually active by the time they get to high school, which will then benefit your client. (If nothing else, this activity should reveal the thinking behind some of the ads your kids see in magazines.) You should then have your staff (the students) advise you on the best strategies they could recommend to encourage junior highers to have sex. What you are likely to get in response are the temptations that most affect your group members. Afterward, explain that many junior highers might not be having sex simply because the right opportunity hasn't come along yet. Make sure your kids are willing to fight off lustful thoughts for the right reasons—not simply because they have nothing to worry about yet.

Step 3

As you discuss Jesus' command to avoid lust, ask: **How do you think Jesus avoided lust? After all, He was followed around by many appreciative women whom He had healed or helped in some way. Prostitutes anointed His feet with perfume and used their hair to dry them. The Pharisees tried to trip Him up by bringing before Him a woman caught in adultery—who was possibly still naked. Jesus had a human body, just like the rest of us. How do you think He kept from lusting after all of these women?** After some discussion, kids should realize that Jesus never judged people on outward appearance. Rather, He saw past the physical aspects of people and saw them as spiritual children of His heavenly Father. We can do the same thing. It's hard and it takes a lot of practice, but we'll form stronger friendships as we are able to get past the outer (sexual?) attractions to other people and truly care about them as fellow, struggling, human beings.

Step 5

As you deal with the ways that people try to avoid lusting after others, challenge group members by turning the question around. Say: **Tell the truth. Do you ever want to be lusted after? This isn't an easy question. Where do we draw the lines between having a positive self-image and a need for others to like us? When we're picking clothes, getting ready in the morning, and going through our regular grooming activities, what do we have in mind? Do we want to look attractive? Do we want to look "hot"? Do we even know?** It could be that some of your kids have less of a need to avoid lusting after others and more of a need to keep from trying to become an *object* of lust. Peter's words in 1 Peter 3:3, 4 are addressed to wives, but should apply to all of us in today's culture.

Date Used:

	Approx. Time
Step 1: The Great Cover-Up	_____ 5
o Extra Action	
o Large Group	
o Mostly Guys	
o Short Meeting Time	
Things needed:	
Step 2: The Fine Line of Lust	Urban 5-10
o Large Group	
o Heard It All Before	
o Mostly Guys	
o Extra Fun	
o Media	
o Short Meeting Time	
o Urban	
Things needed:	
Step 3: What's Love Got to Do with It?	E. C. 20
o Small Group	
o Heard It All Before	
o Little Bible Background	
o Fellowship & Worship	
o Mostly Girls	
o Combined Junior High/High School	
o Extra Challenge	
Things needed:	
Step 4: Lustbusters	_____ 15
o Extra Action	
o Mostly Girls	
o Urban	
o Combined Junior High/High School	
Things needed:	
Step 5: You Can Do It	E. C. 15
o Small Group	Bble
o Little Bible Background	
o Fellowship & Worship	
o Extra Fun	
o Media	
o Extra Challenge	
Things needed:	

Are Mountain-Moving Prayers Possible?

YOUR GOALS FOR THIS SESSION:

Choose one or more

☐ To help kids gain new insights into prayer.

☐ To help kids understand why some prayers may seem to go unanswered.

☐ To help kids persist in prayer for some unresolved issues.

☐ Other _____

Your Bible Base:

Matthew 17:14-20
Luke 11:5-13
James 4:3
1 John 5:14, 15

Word Pictures

(Needed: Copies of Repro Resource 2, pencils)

Before the session you'll need to make several copies of "Fractured Answers" (Repro Resource 2). Cut most of the sheets in half lengthwise and discard the right side. But be sure to keep several whole sheets for a charade activity.

Have group members form teams of four. Explain that the teams will be competing in a charade activity. Ask each team to choose one member to act out the charade and another to record the team's answers.

Give team members copies of the left side of Repro Resource 2. Then gather the "actors" from each team together and give them full copies of Repro Resource 2. Explain that they are to act out each phrase ("wet behind the ears," "rub my nose in it," etc.) for their team-mates. They may not say anything to their teammates or even mouth words, but must act out the meaning of the words. As a last resort, they may act out words that sound like the words in the phrase. (The "sounds like" signal is pulling on the ear.)

Send the "actors" back to their teams to begin. The first team to guess its actor's clues and complete the four clichés wins.

Afterward, ask: **What do all these phrases that were acted out have in common—"wet behind the ears," "rub my nose in it," "the straw that broke the camel's back," and "risen to new heights"?** (They're all clichés, metaphors, and figurative ways of saying things.)

Explain: **Today's tough passage is tough not only because it talks about how to do the impossible, but because it's also written in figurative language.**

Have group members turn in their Bibles to Matthew 17:20. Ask a volunteer to read it aloud.

Then say: **Jesus wasn't saying that Christians are supposed to go up to mountains and say, "Hey, take a swim." What do you think He was saying?** (Through prayer, Christians can accomplish great things.)

In New Testament times, people used figurative language or metaphors to describe their great teachers who could explain difficulties. They called these teachers "uprooters" of mountains, much the way today we call people who get

things done "movers and shakers."

Ask: **How much faith did Jesus say you needed to be a spiritual "mover and shaker"?** (Not much—"faith as small a mustard seed," which is very small.)

How does this fact make you feel? Some group members may feel empowered that such a small faith can produce so much. Others may feel ashamed that they don't have even that much faith. Still others may be bewildered because their small faith does not seem to produce these dramatic results.

S.O.S. Prayer Requests

(Needed: Copies of Repro Resource 3, pencils)

Explain: **This verse about moving mountains with a small amount of faith makes some people wonder why their small faith doesn't seem to do much good. Let's look at some of the prayers you may have prayed that may or may not have been answered.**

Distribute copies of "Everyday Teen Prayers" (Repro Resource 3) and pencils. Read aloud the instructions. Then give an example of a substitution for the first prayer (e.g., "that the car keys I locked in the car would miraculously appear in my pocket") to give group members an idea of what you're looking for.

Give group members a few minutes to work. When they're finished, ask volunteers to share some of their responses.

Then say: **This list mentions a few serious matters such as gangs and getting along with parents. What are some other serious items that you've prayed for? Have they been answered?** If possible, try to remember group members' responses. You can refer to them later in the session.

Clues to Unanswered Prayer

(Needed: Bibles, chalkboard and chalk or newsprint and marker)

Say: **When our prayers aren't answered the way we want them answered, it's easy to feel disappointed with God. It's also easy to feel disappointed in our own faith—that it's so small we can't move a mountain, or even a molehill! That's how the disciples felt when Jesus told them about the power of prayer.**

Have someone read aloud Matthew 17:14-20. Then explain the background for this incident: **The disciples had failed to cast out a demon because they lacked faith. Jesus tried to inspire them, to give them hope. With just a little faith, He said, they could do great things!**

Write the following question on the board: "Why do some prayers seem to go unanswered?"

Have group members form three teams (perhaps the same teams you used for the charades game in Step 1). Assign each team one of the following Scripture passages: James 4:3; I John 5:14, 15; Luke 11:5-13. Instruct the teams to look up their assigned passages to find clues to the question on the board.

Give the teams a few minutes to work. When they're finished, have each one share its clue. Write the clues on the board as teams share them. Use the following suggestions to supplement the teams' responses.

- Clue #1: Some requests are made with wrong motives (James 4:3).
- Clue #2: Some requests don't follow God's will (I John 5:14, 15).
- Clue #3: Sometimes God wants to teach us something by making us wait—but that doesn't mean we shouldn't keep asking with boldness (Luke 11:5-13).

Use the following information to guide your discussion of the three assigned Scripture passages.

For James 4:3: **Some prayers are unwise. We pray with wrong motives, focusing on our own pleasure and disregarding what others need. This may explain why the disciples' faith was not strong enough to cast out the demon** (Matthew 17:16). **Perhaps their motives were impure and they were "showing off" God's power.**

What kinds of prayers probably aren't answered because

they're asked with the wrong motives? (Prayers for luxuries and riches so that we will feel better about ourselves, so that we can impress others, or so that we won't have to work hard, etc.)

Point out that this doesn't mean God doesn't want people to enjoy themselves; but self-indulgence makes a person self-centered. Self-centeredness taints our relationships and takes our focus off God's purpose in our lives.

For I John 5:14, 15: **This is similar to the problem of having mixed motives. God is eager to give us what we want, but He wants us to seek His will.**

How can we know what God's will is? (The simplest way to define His will is by the clear commands of Scripture.)

Point out that the two greatest commandments are to love God and to love others (Matthew 22:37-40). As Jesus said, these two commands sum up all the law and the prophets.

What kinds of prayers probably aren't answered because they violate these two commandments? (Requests that would harm others, requests that would lead to sexual impurity or other sin, requests that are selfish, etc.)

For Luke 11:5-13: **This passage may provide the best answer to our question; but it, too, is difficult. Jesus is not saying that God is like the grouchy neighbor who doesn't want to be bothered, though sometimes it may seem like it. Jesus tells the disciples to ask, to seek, and even to knock if they have to in order to get what they want. In other words, keep praying. Don't give up. You will get what you ask for, and even more, if you keep on praying.**

What kinds of things might God be able to teach us by making us wait for the answer to a sincere prayer? (He can teach us patience and faith. He can help us learn about ourselves—what's really important to us that we're not willing to give up on. He can teach us about Himself. He might not give us what we thought we wanted, but He could give us a better relationship with Himself.)

What kinds of prayers do we often have to wait to see answered? (Prayers for someone's salvation, prayers for relationships, prayers for personal growth, prayers for understanding for why something has happened, prayers for health concerns, etc.)

Ask: **Is it possible that we don't see our prayers answered because we give up too soon?** Get a few responses.

If you have time, offer one other explanation for prayers that seem to go unanswered. Explain: **God will not violate a person's free will on behalf of another person. In other words, we can't change others or force them to do certain things just by praying. People can choose whether or not to accept Christ, or to like you or not like you. God will not allow us to use prayer and faith as "weapons" to control others.**

— Prayers that seem to be according to G's will, yet unanswered.

↳ 2 things I know:

① G told me to pray & that he will answer

② G is in control.

— faith in midst of "impossibility" ↳ mustard seed.

What kinds of prayers seem to go unanswered because people exercise their free will against God's will? (Prayers that nations will not attack each other in war, prayers for safety—people endanger their own lives and others by being careless, prayers that family members will make peace with each other, etc.)

Explain: **Even though God will not violate another person's free will, He does influence people. And we must remember that He is ultimately in control. Despite what anybody else does or doesn't do, God will accomplish His purposes. Our prayers are a part of that process—otherwise He wouldn't have commanded us to pray.**

[handwritten notes in right margin:]
— Mark 9 story
What are some things that help our faith grow? Answer to prayer. what begets answer to prayer? action? — Steve + Sonie Sarah

STEP 4

Practice Prayers

(Needed: Chalkboard and chalk or newsprint and marker, a hand-held weight, copies of Repro Resource 3)

Hold up a hand-held weight. Ask: **Which comes first—the ability to lift a weight or the muscles to do it? I could say that I can't lift weights because I don't have enough muscles. I could also say that I don't have muscles because I don't lift weights. The truth is that the two build each other. As you lift weights, your muscles gain strength. As your muscles gain strength, you can lift more weights. Prayer and faith are the same way. Prayer builds faith and faith builds prayer. You keep practicing and working out, and they both grow.**

Let's look again at some of the requests on the "Everyday Teen Prayers" handout. The clues on the board help us see that we need to examine our motives, make sure that what we're asking for is in accordance with God's will, be persistent in our prayers, and remember that other people have free wills of their own.

Focus group members' attention on some of the following requests from Repro Resource 3 or on some of the requests group members mentioned at the end of Step 2.

Ask: **What would a prayer of faith sound like for this request?**

• *Request #3: That I'll make the final cut for the basketball team.* ("Lord, I need Your guidance. Will it help me or hurt me to be a part of

OPTIONS panel (left margin):
HEARD IT ALL BEFORE
FELLOWSHIP & WORSHIP
MOSTLY GIRLS
MOSTLY GUYS
MEDIA
EXTRA CHALLENGE

the basketball team? Is this an ego trip? Do I want this because it could help me get a scholarship to college or because I just plain enjoy it? It would help me stay fit, but how will I react if I don't make it? Lord, I want Your will in this.")

• *Request #4: That a certain person of the opposite sex would notice me.* ("Show me, God, if this person would be a good influence on me. If so, how could I serve this person instead of hoping he or she will make me look good to others or feel good about myself? Help this person follow Your will too. If this person would not be good for me, please help me give up my feelings for him or her.")

• *Request #7: That a hot car would appear in my driveway tomorrow for me.* ("Lord, You know how much I want a car. If I had a nice car, I would want to use it to serve You. But I know that it would also be an ego trip to impress others. Help me be content with what I have and trust You to meet all my needs.")

• *Request #9: That a friend who's been ignoring me will want to be friends again.* ("Show me, Lord, if I've offended my friend. Do I have any attitudes that hurt other people? If my friend is going through troubles, help me figure out how to be his or her friend without being a pest. If this friend keeps ignoring me, help me to get over the hurt and find other friends.")

• *Request #10: That I would get along better with my parents.* ("God, help me to try to be more respectful to my parents even when we disagree. Help me explain my position calmly and not resent them or get mad at them. Help them give me a break, to see that I want to try to get along with them.")

The Pause That Refreshes

Close the session with a time of prayer. Say: **Think of something you've prayed for that seems to have gone unanswered. Or maybe you haven't formally prayed for it, but you've wished for it.** Give group members a minute or two to think. **Consider the reasons on the board why prayers don't seem to be answered and pray again about this issue.**

Allow a few minutes of quiet time for prayer. Then close by praying aloud, asking God to help you and your group members bring your requests to Him, remaining open to His will and His answers to prayer.

Fractured Answers

1

What's wrong with that new cook? Can't he fry burgers?

REPLY: No, he's ...

1

wet behind the ears.

2

You sure did a bad job!

REPLY: Don't ...

2

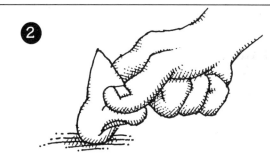

rub my nose in it!

3

I'm sorry I dropped your mirror and spilled your styling gel. Now I've broken your hair dryer too.

REPLY: That's the ...

3

straw that broke the camel's back.

4

I knew she liked to study, but I can't believe she's going to be valedictorian.

REPLY: Yes, she's ...

4

risen to new heights.

Everyday **Teen** Prayers

Check the prayers below that you've prayed. Below the ones you don't check, write the closest thing to it that you've prayed.

_____ 1. That my lost contact lens would miraculously reappear in the soap dish after gurgling down the drain.
Similar prayer: _____
_____

_____ 2. That I would instantly understand everything I didn't learn in Algebra I so I can understand Algebra II.
Similar prayer:_____
_____

_____ 3. That I'll make the final cut for the basketball team.
Similar prayer: _____
_____

_____ 4. That a certain person of the opposite sex would notice me.
Similar prayer: _____
_____

_____ 5. That a zit would disappear overnight.
Similar prayer: _____
_____

_____ 6. That a younger brother or sister would disappear overnight.
Similar prayer: _____
_____

_____ 7. That a hot car would appear in my driveway tomorrow for me.
Similar prayer: _____
_____

_____ 8. That I would be safe from gang activity.
Similar prayer: _____
_____

_____ 9. That a friend who's been ignoring me will want to be friends again.
Similar prayer:_____
_____

_____ 10. That I would get along better with my parents.
Similar prayer: _____
_____

EXTRA ACTION

Step 1

To begin the session, have group members form two or three teams for a relay. At one end of a large room or open area, pile up a large stack of assorted junk. Some things should be small and others large—but not so large that they couldn't be picked up by all group members. (All you need to do is clean out a closet and pile up the items you take out.) Teams should line up, single file, parallel to each other, across the length of the room. At your signal, the teams should try to move the stack of stuff from one end of the room to the other by picking up one item at a time and passing it, fire-brigade style, to the other end. Each team should maintain a stack separate from the others' at the other side of the room. After several minutes, stop and check to see who has the largest pile and/or the most items. Refer to this exercise when you get to the verse about moving mountains, and explain that there's an easier way.

Step 2

Begin this step by dividing members into teams. Have each team write and perform a skit. The theme of the skit should be "You never listen to me!" The teams may do anything they want for that theme. Some skits may deal with parents, friends, brothers and sisters, teachers, and so forth. Although the skits will probably contain a lot of humor, you should also be able to detect students' *feelings* when they sense they aren't being heard. This information will be valuable as you approach the topic of unanswered prayer. If they feel bad when they feel ignored by someone they love, how do they feel when they think God is ignoring them?

SMALL GROUP

Step 1

To help emphasize the "faith the size of a mustard seed" concept, bring a variety of fruits and vegetables (and possibly flowers). Have each group member take a different fruit or vegetable, dig out a few of the seeds, and show the size difference among the seeds. In some cases the difference won't be phenomenal (in a blackberry, for instance). In other cases, there will be major size differences. (Try to have on hand some sunflower seeds, acorns, or pecans and discuss the potential of such seeds.) Explain that it would be easy enough to eat or disregard the seeds. But if they are planted, with a bit of faith and a long period of patient waiting, they will produce large, delicious fruit. Apply this concept not only to prayer, but to your group as well. Emphasize that being small in size (or numbers) is not necessarily good or bad in itself. More important is what you do as a small group and the attitudes you have as you wait for growth.

Step 3

Instead of breaking into even smaller groups to study the Bible passages, go through them together. Just be sure everyone stays involved and is not allowed to sit back while other people answer all of the questions. One way to keep everyone in the discussion is to use group members' names when you refer to various prayers. If it's Denny's prayer that a hot car appear in his driveway or Belinda's desire that a certain guy would notice her, the session will take on a more personal appeal. And just hearing their names being used will usually pull most people out of their daydreams and back into reality.

LARGE GROUP

Step 1

To introduce the topic of prayer, say: **True or false—Large groups don't need to be quite as devoted to prayer as small groups. After all, if we need a mountain moved, we can usually shovel it away ourselves or hold a fund-raiser to get it done.** Most kids will say that the answer is false. But challenge them to prove it. Can they think of a time when one person's small prayer was more powerful than the actions of another large group? (They might recall Moses at the Red Sea as God took the Israelites safely through while the Egyptians drowned [Exodus 14:13-31]; Elijah and the priests of Baal [I Kings 18:25-40]; etc.) Explain that perhaps the main obstacle to effective prayer is trying to handle things on our own. Sometimes in a large group, that tendency is even stronger than in other groups. Challenge group members to think in terms of their one-on-one relationship with God during the rest of the session.

Step 3

Think of a simple trick that anyone can do if he or she knows the "secret"; but choose one that most of your group members won't know. One simple trick is the "magnetic" Bic pen. Hold a Bic pen in one hand and the pointed cap in the other. Slowly bring them closer together. As soon as they get close, the cap "magically" leaps onto the pen with considerable force. (With a bit of saliva on the thumb and forefinger holding the cap, and a squeeze, the cap will shoot out of your hand and onto the pen.) Pass the "magic" pen around and see how many people have the same "power" you have. Point out that it can be embarrassing to be in front of a large group and fail to figure out some simple thing that someone else can do easily. Tie this into how the disciples might have felt when they publicly failed to cast out the demon that Jesus removed at once. Explain that kids can avoid that powerless feeling if they begin to establish a direct link to God through prayer.

Step 3

To help your kids understand why God may not answer prayer as we wish He would (even though they may assume they know), preface the discussion with a skit. Group members should act as a group of kids who have come to a Christian conference to spend the weekend, hear some speakers and musicians, and get to know each other better. They've just arrived, and this is the first time they've seen each other. Hand out slips of paper to assign different roles for kids to play. One person's paper should say, "You desperately want to make friends with these people. Your goal is to spend quality time with every person while you're here." All of the other papers should say things like "You've been up all night for the past three days, studying for exams, and you're desperately tired." "You're in a coma." "You were forced to come here. You don't like Christians or anything they stand for." Begin the roleplay and watch as one person tries to communicate with the others. Afterward, explain that sometimes there are perfectly good reasons why other people don't respond to us in the way we expect. The same is true of prayer. We may expect a certain answer from God, but He may have a good reason not to respond as we anticipated.

Step 4

Demonstrate the need for commitment not only to individual growth, but to the group as well. Have one of the largest kids in the group sit in a chair. Then ask the smallest person to pick him up—chair and all. After he or she attempts this, add another small person. Let the two struggle. Then add a third, and so on. Show that as you keep adding people, the job becomes less of a hassle—and maybe even more fun. Emphasize that, while individual spiritual growth (and prayer) is very important, we can draw a lot of support from other people as well. We need to pray for them and help them pray for us by sharing our needs, hopes, and dreams.

Step 1

It's likely that group members who have only a little Bible background may find it particularly hard to comprehend the figurative language of being able to "move mountains" with prayer. However, in this case, you can help them by referring them to a phrase they may be more familiar with: "making mountains out of molehills." Discuss the meaning of the familiar expression. Then explain that Jesus was trying to show us the other side of the expression. We do tend to make mountains out of molehills in many areas of our lives. But with prayer, we can make mountains *into* molehills. Worry exaggerates out problems. Prayer reduces them down to a manageable size—because we trust God to do the managing instead of ourselves. Be sensitive throughout this session for phrases that may seem quite natural in Christian circles—but that may seem strange or incomprehensible for some of your group members.

Step 3

When you get to the "clues" as to why God may not answer prayers, slow down and take your time with the section. It's more important that your group members understand these concepts than that you get finished with the session. On one hand, you're telling them that sometimes God has good reasons for not answering us as we wish He would. On the other hand, you're telling them to pray persistently and with all of the faith they can muster. You're right in both cases, but a person new to Christian teaching may not see the logic in repeated praying and steadfast faith if God has good reasons not to answer. Provide a lot of time to encourage questions during this portion of the session.

Step 4

Have your group members do a bit of self-evaluation when they get to this step. Since "prayer builds faith, and faith builds prayer," it is important to continue to develop both. Ask: **In your own life, which would you say is stronger—your faith or your prayer life?** Give kids time to think about it and respond. Then put the strong-faith people in one group and the strong-prayer people in another. Let those who can't decide go to the group with fewer people. Ask each group to compose a list of guidelines that would help the other group. (The prayer people should do a "Tips for More Effective Praying" list to give the faith people, and the faith people should do a "Tips for Building Stronger Faith" list for the prayer people.) Lists should include hints that members can attest to from personal experience as well as other things they know to be true from Scripture or previous teaching. During the next week, make copies of both lists to hand out to everyone as you challenge group members to "build up their muscles" in both of these areas.

Step 5

One of the worst things you can do is talk about prayer all the way through this session and then quickly close in prayer as you normally do—without any practical application of what you've been talking about. Encourage everyone to take part in the closing, even if he or she says just a sentence prayer. If nothing else, kids should be able to express thanks for something they learned during the session. In that case, part of the prayer might focus on how we can benefit when God answers prayer; another part might focus on how we can benefit when God *doesn't* answer prayer as we expect. In either case, we can always count on God's faithfulness to us, and should take plenty of time to express our thanks to Him.

Step 2

After your group members respond to "Everyday Teen Prayers" (Repro Resource 3), ask them to think of questions they've had about prayer in the last few years. Have them try to remember how they understood prayer or felt about praying when they were young children. See if they can recite any prayers that they learned as children, like "Now I lay me down to sleep . . ." Then ask: **What is different about your concept of prayer now? What are your questions about prayer now?**

Step 4

Ask your group members to form teams of four to discuss the following questions: **"Is my faith in my ability to pray or in God and His power? What difference would it make either way?"** Give the teams a few minutes to discuss their responses; then have them share what they discussed.

Step 3

As you discuss God's responses to our requests, be particularly sensitive to the fact that many people—perhaps guys more than girls—tend to see their heavenly Father in much the same way that they see their human fathers. Guys who've been pushing for more privileges, or who may be going through a rebellious stage, could at this point in their lives have a strained relationship with their fathers. They may be told no quite often when they ask for things. As a result, they may come to expect the same tension any time they ask God for something. Ask: **How do your parents usually respond when you ask them for something out of the ordinary? What's the most unusual request you've made of them lately? What's the most unusual request you've made of God lately? Do you make assumptions about God based on the responses of your parents? If so, in what ways?** If you don't deal openly with these issues, your guys may interpret many of the comments in this session as a spiritual version of "Because I said so, that's why!" Do what you can to make a distinction between an all-knowing, all-loving God and our human, fallible, imperfect parents.

Step 4

Say: **Be completely honest here. What would you be most proud of— a very strong and muscular body, or a very strong and productive prayer life? Why?** Let guys respond. Then ask: **Does prayer sometimes seem a bit "feminine" or "wimpy" to you? Do you usually pray for everything you need, or mostly for the things you know you can't get on your own? Do you really believe Jesus when He says that strength comes from prayer?** Try to detect any underlying attitudes that prayer is a "last resort" or that "real men don't pray." Emphasize that prayer is the only constant source of real strength—for any person in any situation.

Step 3

Sometime during this step you might find it effective to play "Gossip." Have group members sit in a circle. Whisper a message into the ear of one person. (The message should be written, word for word, on a piece of paper.) The message should then be whispered, person to person, around the room. A person may not repeat the message after he or she has said it once. Each person must pass along exactly what he or she thinks he or she hears. When the message gets to the last person, have him or her say it aloud. Then compare it to what was written on the paper. Most of the time the message will be considerably different, and you can backtrack to see where it got distorted. This exercise can point out that sometimes a message (or perhaps an answer to prayer) can start out clear, but become distorted by other noise or circumstances so that we misunderstand what is being said.

Step 5

Wrap up the session with all of your group members (except for the smallest guy) sitting in a circle on the floor, close enough together for all of their feet to touch in the center as they extend their legs. The smallest guy should stand in the center of the circle with the others' feet pushed up tight against him. The center person should then hold his hands to his side, make his body stiff, and topple in the direction of his choice. The other group members should be close enough to reach out and keep him from falling, passing him on to others in the group. With some practice, a group can get a person spinning around the circle pretty fast. Point out that as your center person learns to trust the others, the experience can be thrilling. So it is with God. As we learn to trust Him more completely when we come to Him in prayer, our lives take on a new vitality.

Step 3

In conjunction with the Bible study teams, have group members suppose they are reporters for a first-century tabloid, *The Jerusalem Tattler.* Ask them to create attention-grabbing headlines for the passages they are studying (James 4:3; I John 5:14, 15; and Luke 11:5-13). You can use the passage you already covered (Matthew 17:14-20) to practice with. Some examples might include:
• "Lose Tons in Just Days with New, Mountain-Moving Prayer Diet"
• "Amazing Mustard Seed Miracle Cure for Demon Possession"
• "Country Preacher's Astounding Claim: Nothing Is Impossible!"

Point out that many tabloid stories miss the point and don't quite print the truth. So in each case, the headlines can be a bit exaggerated (after all, they need to sell papers), but teams should also be able to cite all of the facts as well.

Step 4

Follow up on the "muscle development" theme in this step. Put together a workout video that would help others tone up flabby spiritual muscles. Work together as a group on the project. Some group members will need to determine what exercises need to be done and how often they should be repeated for proper strength. Others will need to actually demonstrate the exercises on camera. Still others should be responsible for the taping, lighting, and other technical aspects of the video (assuming you have access to a video camera). You might also want to think about appropriate "celebrities" (prominent pray-ers in your church or community) who might endorse or participate in the video. Have some fun with this, and the kids will remember the point of the exercise far longer than a traditional lecture or discussion.

Step 2

Give a brief introduction and start the session with Repro Resource 3. When students finish, let volunteers share some of their responses. As you move into Step 3, you can save a lot of time by summarizing the Bible content rather than dividing into teams to discuss it and report back. Consequently, you should still have plenty of time to do Steps 4 and 5, focusing on improving and practicing prayer habits.

Step 3

Another effective session shortcut is to simply do Steps 3 and 5. With this option, you might also want to open the session with Repro Resource 3. By the time your students work through the handout, divide into groups, discuss the Bible content, and report back, you should have just enough time to discuss the application material at the end of Step 3 and in Step 5.

Step 3

Try using skits to communicate that prayer is personal conversation with God and that it requires our listening. Ask for volunteers to perform the following three skits:
• *Skit 1*—A kid has a question that only God can answer. While the kid ponders the question, a phone rings. On the other end of the line is God, calling to answer the kid's question. The tension of the skit lies in the fact that the kid can't decide whether to answer the phone or not. The point is that when God calls us with answers, the decision to respond to Him is often left up to the individual.
• *Skit 2*—A kid has a crisis at 4 A.M. and is trying to call someone for help. He or she calls friends, his or her pastor, etc., but everyone is too sleepy to offer immediate help. Finally, the person calls God, who is wide awake and more than willing to help. The point is that we can call God at any time.
• *Skit 3*—A kid is facing an issue in which he or she needs advice from God. The kid calls God several times for advice; but each time God starts to respond, the kid hangs up, thinking he or she has just come up with a solution on his or her own. The point is that it's no good to call God (pray) if we're not willing to listen or take the time to hear the answer God gives.

Step 5

Have your teens include their own city in their prayers. Before praying, discuss some of the "mountains" that need to be moved in the city—problems that seem impossible to overcome. Your list will probably include things like crime, drugs, violence, racism, broken families, gangs, and AIDS. This list should help your group members pray more specifically.

Step 1

Consider the maturity level of your group members before you even begin this session. Many junior highers may need a basic session on "What is prayer?" "How do you pray?" and "What's the big deal about praying?" before they're ready to try to move mountains. Ask: **If you knew a person you really liked who could protect you from bullies, give you neat stuff that you couldn't afford on your own, offer good advice to help you make hard decisions, and was willing to be your friend, would you want to develop the relationship? Why? How much time every day do you think you would spend with this person?** Explain that God more than fulfills these criteria for us, and that prayer is one of the major ways we spend time with Him. After you help your junior highers focus more on the importance of getting started with regular, personal prayer, then move on to Repro Resource 3 and the rest of the session.

Step 3

Instead of dealing with the mountain-moving power of prayer, save that concept for later. Ask: **Does God answer every single one of your prayers?** Let kids respond. **Why do you think some prayers go unanswered?** Have group members examine the Bible texts (James 4:3; I John 5:14, 15; and Luke 11:5-13) together rather than in teams. You should guide the discussion and answer any questions kids might have. Then *close* with the mountain-moving concept, which should be an encouragement to younger and smaller members. After showing the importance of prayer, and the power that comes with more faithful praying, challenge your students to get more involved with regularly scheduled periods of prayer.

Step 4

As you discuss the faith-prayer cycle and how the two are related, have someone read aloud Mark's version of the story of the man whose son had an evil spirit (Mark 9:14-29). Discuss the passage as a group, focusing on Jesus' words to the boy's father and the father's response. See if anyone else feels the same way as the father (who replied, "I do believe; help me overcome my unbelief!"). Ask: **What does it mean to believe, but to experience unbelief at the same time?** (Perhaps some people believe God is *capable* of doing anything, but not particularly interested in doing it for *them*.) Tie in this response to the need for strengthening our faith "muscles" and becoming stronger as we keep "working out."

Step 5

In some cases, we may overlook the importance of prayer simply because we take so much answered prayer for granted. Maybe we only notice the times that God *doesn't* answer as we had hoped. If so, consider beginning a prayer journal for your group. At each meeting, ask for prayer requests and write them down, with the date. As prayers are answered, record those dates as well (and continue praying for the yet unanswered requests). Also keep up with notes of thanksgiving, which should be included in your prayers as well. Before long, your group members should be able to look back and see an intensely active God who plays a regular role in providing for their needs, helping them through hard times, and allowing them to experience truly abundant lives.

Date Used:

Approx.
Time

Step 1: Word Pictures _____
o Extra Action
o Small Group
o Large Group
o Little Bible Background
o Combined Junior High/High School
Things needed:

Step 2: S.O.S. Prayer Requests _____
o Extra Action
o Mostly Girls
o Short Meeting Time
Things needed:

Step 3: Clues to Unanswered Prayer _____
o Small Group
o Large Group
o Heard It All Before
o Little Bible Background
o Mostly Guys
o Extra Fun
o Media
o Short Meeting Time
o Urban
o Combined Junior High/High School
Things needed:

Step 4: Practice Prayers _____
o Heard It All Before
o Fellowship & Worship
o Mostly Girls
o Mostly Guys
o Media
o Extra Challenge
Things needed:

Step 5: The Pause That Refreshes _____
o Fellowship & Worship
o Extra Fun
o Urban
o Extra Challenge
Things needed:

What, Me Worry?

YOUR GOALS FOR THIS SESSION:

Choose one or more

☐ To help kids discover what God says about seeking His kingdom instead of worrying about the future.

☐ To help kids understand that there is a balance between proper planning and worry.

☐ To help kids choose not to worry about things over which they have no control.

☐ Other _____
_____

Your Bible Base:

Proverbs 6:6-11
Matthew 6:25-34

The Blindfold Conspiracy

(Needed: Chalkboard and chalk or newsprint and marker, blindfolds)

Ask three or four volunteers to write a list of their five favorite music groups (or some other list of five or more things) on the board while they are blindfolded. Explain that the winner is the person whose list has the straightest left margin. If the margins are equally straight, the first one finished wins.

Blindfold the volunteers. Quietly whisper to one of them that you're going to remove his or her blindfold. Motion to the rest of the group not to say anything as you do so.

Say: **Ready, set, go!** Have the volunteers write their lists. When they're finished, have them all remove their blindfolds. Judge the columns. The contestant who wasn't blindfolded probably will have the straightest left column. Declare him or her the winner.

Afterward, explain to the rest of the contestants what you did. Then ask: **Why was it easier for the person who wasn't blindfolded to win?** (He or she could see what he or she was doing.)

What advantage was there in being able to see the board? (It gives the writer more control.)

Explain that today's "tough teaching" is about worry: "Do not worry about tomorrow, for tomorrow will worry about itself" (Matthew 6:34). Read the verse aloud.

Then say: **This brings up a lot of questions: How can I not worry when the world is in such a mess? Am I supposed to expect the things I need to drop out of the sky? If I don't plan for the future, won't I end up starving or homeless?**

No matter how hard the blindfolded people tried, they really couldn't make a straight list because they couldn't see the whole picture. In the same way, none of us can see the whole picture of our lives. We don't know what's going to happen tomorrow. But we have an advantage over other "blindfolded people." We know someone who *can* see the whole picture. God has no blindfold on.

STEP 2

Why Worry Shouldn't Win

(Needed: Bibles, pencils, copies of Repro Resource 4)

Have group members turn in their Bibles to Matthew 6:25-34. Distribute copies of "The Super-Duper, In-Depth Quiz for Astute Kids" (Repro Resource 4) and pencils. Instruct group members to complete the multiple-choice quiz, using Matthew 6:25-34 as a guide.

Give group members a few minutes to work. When they're finished, go through the answers one at a time. Use the following information to supplement group members' responses.

(1) b. Verse 25 says not to worry about your life (what you eat and drink) or your body (what you will wear).

(2) b. See verses 31 and 32.

(3) c. Verse 28 says the lilies do not labor or spin, but God still takes care of them—and we are more valuable than they are.

(4) b and c. Verse 34 teaches us to face our problems one day at a time. We should do what we can do about today and not worry about every little detail of the future. Verse 33 offers another reason not to worry about tomorrow: God provides the necessities.

(5) b. Verse 33 talks about seeking God's kingdom and righteousness, and trusting God to provide "all these things" (the necessities of life). Helping to supply basic necessities for others is commanded, and enjoying one's self is encouraged in other Bible passages, but they aren't mentioned here. (See I John 3:17 and Ecclesiastes 3:1-8.)

Ask: **What does it mean to seek God's kingdom?** (To do His will, to acknowledge Him as Master and Lord.)

What does it mean to "seek . . . [God's] righteousness"? Get a few responses. Then explain: **To seek God's righteousness means to desire to do the right thing, for the right reason. God is the only one who is truly righteous, but He commands us to be righteous as well** (Leviticus 19:2). **Therefore we must seek His power to help us live righteously.**

(6) c. In verse 27, Jesus asks (tongue in cheek) if worrying does any good. Can it add even one measly hour to our lives? Yet some people like to worry. They figure maybe bad things won't happen if they worry and suffer enough.

Say: **The command not to worry about tomorrow may sound to some as though Jesus was telling people not to plan for the future at all. But the Bible never contradicts itself,**

OPTIONS

SMALL GROUP

LARGE GROUP

HEARD IT ALL BEFORE

LITTLE BIBLE BACKGROUND

FELLOWSHIP & WORSHIP

MOSTLY GUYS

EXTRA FUN

SHORT MEETING TIME

EXTRA CHALLENGE

and other passages tell us about the value of planning ahead. **Proverbs 6:6-11 is one of those passages.**

Have someone read aloud Proverbs 6:6-11. Then say: **It's obvious that the ant wasn't lazy, but there's more than that. What can you learn about life through the ant?** (The ant planned ahead. During summer and fall, it harvested and stashed its food to eat during the winter when food would be scarce. The ant was resourceful. Also, the ant didn't need a boss. It did the job without being told to—it had initiative.)

What do you see as the difference between these two passages? Allow group members to come up with their own conclusions. Then go on to the next activity.

STEP 3

Extreme Thinking

(Needed: Chalkboard and chalk or newsprint and marker)

Draw a horizontal line from one end of the board to the other. Write "Worriers" on one end and "Sluggards" on the other. Draw a center point and some midpoints so that the line looks like a continuum. Point to the word "Worriers" and describe them. Be as extreme and sarcastic as you can.

Perhaps something like the following: **Worriers are sure that someone will figure out the combination to their lockers, break in, and steal their candy bar stash. When their VCRs break down, they don't call a repairman, they call a suicide hot line.**

Point to the word "Sluggards" and describe them similarly: **Sluggards think that their dirty clothes zoom through a secret passage from under their beds to the washing machine, wash themselves, and then zoom back into their drawers. They think that the answers to their homework will miraculously appear if they leave their homework in their locker overnight.**

These are extremes, of course, but tell us where on this continuum you would place yourself. Are you more of a worrier or more of a sluggard? Allow all of your group members to tell you where they fit on the continuum. Make a mark on the board to represent each person. Ask for examples of times group members have either gone too far toward the worry side or too far toward the sluggard side of the continuum.

Say: **God does not want us to worry about tomorrow, but that's not an excuse to be lazy and make no plans either. What He does want us to do is trust Him.**

Write the word "Trust" in the middle of your continuum between "Worriers" and "Sluggards." Then say: **What Jesus was really trying to get at is "What is your ultimate goal in life?" We don't need to be obsessed or worried about the necessities of life. God knows we need those things. One of the things that should make a disciple of Jesus Christ different from a non-Christian** (the "pagans" in the Matthew passage) **is that our goal in life should not be our own financial security or status. We can trust that God will take care of us. We should not be foolish like the sluggard, but we don't have to be obsessed about material things either.**

STEP 4

Getting Concrete

Briefly discuss how the Matthew 6 and Proverbs 6 passages could apply to various things in your group members' lives such as getting good grades, buying a car, deciding on a career, deciding whether or whom to marry, going shopping, etc.

Ask: **Where does normal, constructive planning leave off and obsession begin? On the other hand, when does trusting God for our needs leave off and being a sluggard begin?** These are tough issues. Your group members will probably come up with different answers.

To get this discussion going with concrete examples, start with a for-instance such as what to do with your summer. Ask: **What should be the first step in figuring out what you're going to do with your summer?**

There are probably three general kinds of things group members might think of doing with their summers. One is fun and recreation. They might plan some kind of trip or anticipate spending as much time as possible at the beach, in the mountains, or doing some kind of recreation. Another obvious thing is to find a job to help save money for college, a car, etc. A third option would be to spend the summer, or

OPTIONS

LARGE GROUP

HEARD IT ALL BEFORE

MOSTLY GUYS

URBAN

JR.HIGH HIGH SCHOOL COMBINED

part of it, in some kind of mission or service project. Many kids may think about doing all three.

It is hoped they will see that the first thing they should do with this kind of a decision is to seek God's kingdom. In other words, to pray and ask God what *He* wants them to do with their summer.

Make sure you point out that God is not against us having fun, so thinking about recreation is not necessarily selfish—unless that's our first, and perhaps only, priority.

God is also not against making money. Getting a job may be the most responsible thing we could do. But it could also be a selfish goal.

Participating in some kind of service, going to camp, or taking advantage of some other opportunity for spiritual enrichment or mission is a good idea for most people at some time in their lives. It's something to consider, but it isn't necessarily the obvious answer to the prayer.

Say: **Suppose you've prayed about it, and you're sure that because of your plans to go to college, you need a job for all or most of the summer. Give an example of someone being a sluggard about getting a summer job.** (Sitting around expecting someone to call you about a job; not checking the want ads; not asking around about what jobs are available; not going out looking and filling out applications; not presenting yourself well in interviews—being late, being sloppily dressed, or acting unconcerned.)

Give an example of someone being obsessive about getting a job to make money over the summer. (Calling fifty times and bugging people for whom you've filled out an application; taking the first offer you get, even though it might not be a good place to work, just because you're scared you won't get another offer; only accepting the highest paying job, or trying to work two or three jobs in order to make as much money as possible; lying on your applications so that you can work more hours or get a job you're not really qualified for; etc.)

Give an example of someone trusting God to meet his or her need for a good summer job. (Filling out applications at as many places as possible; being prepared for interviews by being well-dressed, on time, and polite; weighing the pros and cons of the hours, pay, and environment at various places before you accept a job offer; continuing to seek God's help; etc.)

Afterward, say: **Notice that your motivation is the key. Once that's straight, you do what you can and leave the rest to God. Sometimes that means waiting, and that can be hard.**

STEP 5

Walking Away from Worry

(Needed: Small pieces of paper, pencils, wastebasket)

End the session with a time of reflection and prayer. Distribute a small piece of paper and a pencil to each group member.

Say: **Think about some things in your life that you've been worrying about.** (Responses might include things like whether or not to go to college, getting into the colleges of their choice, buying a car, having the right clothes, not having a girlfriend or boyfriend, etc.)

Are these things you've sought God's opinion on? Remember, prayer is more than just asking for things. It's also a time to consider how God is working in our lives and what He may be leading *us* to do. If this is something *you* need to take action on, write down something you will do about it as God leads.

Have group members fold their papers in half and write the action they need to take on one side.

Then say: **Remember the lists we made at the beginning of the session? It was impossible for those who were blindfolded to make a straight list. They had no control because they couldn't see the whole picture. Think of one or two problems over which you have no control. Write those problems on the other side of your paper. If there's something you do when you start worrying about them that you need to stop, write that as well.**

Instruct group members not to look at each other's papers. After allowing them a few minutes to write, ask them to tear their papers in half, with one side being the action they need to take and other side the things they need to let go of.

Lead the group in prayer, asking God to help group members let go of all the things over which they have no control, and to trust that God will tend to those things and help them stop worrying about them. Also pray that God will help them have the proper balance between trust and good planning.

Ask group members to crumple up the halves of their papers on which they wrote the things they have no control over and throw them into the wastebasket before they leave.

THE SUPER-DUPER
In-Depth Quiz for Astute Kids

Using Matthew 6:25-34 as a guide, answer the following questions. Can more than one answer be correct? It's your call.

1. Jesus said not to worry specifically about …
   a. finding shelter.
   b. what you eat, drink, or wear.
   c. dressing as well as Solomon dressed.
   d. the birds in the air overhead.

2. The pagans "run" after …
   a. other pagans.
   b. food, drink, and clothing.
   c. false ideas.
   d. the birds in the air.

3. The lilies of the field …
   a. do not grow.
   b. do not worry.
   c. do not work.
   d. do not like the birds of the air.

4. You shouldn't worry about tomorrow because …
   a. you can't change what's going to happen anyway.
   b. today gives you enough to worry about.
   c. God will provide the necessities.
   d. there will still be birds in the air, after all.

5. Because God supplies what you need, you should …
   a. try to provide basic necessities for others.
   b. concern yourself with seeking God's kingdom and righteousness.
   c. concern yourself with supplying the luxuries.
   d. kick back and enjoy yourself.

6. Jesus challenged people to question whether worry would …
   a. lead to heart attacks.
   b. give you clothes as cool as Solomon's were.
   c. add an hour on the end of your life.
   d. shoo away the birds of the air.

Step 1

To make the same point as the chalkboard activity while getting more people actively involved, make some "jigsaw puzzles" before the session. The pieces of each puzzle should be identical, which can be accomplished by cutting several sheets of different colored construction paper into small pieces at the same time, then separating the pieces by color. However, one puzzle should be cut from a picture out of a magazine (the same size as the construction paper). Provide an "identical" puzzle for each team or individual in your group. More than likely, the person or team trying to piece together the picture will finish before the students working with the solid colors. You can then make the point that when we are able to see the big picture, we tend to be more successful than when we can't.

Step 5

Rather than merely throwing away the lists of worries over which group members have no control, let group members destroy those worries in a more symbolic way. Each list should be put into a balloon. The balloon should then be blown up (with the list inside), tied at the end, and attached to the person's ankle with a length of string (about twelve to eighteen inches long). Then say (tongue in cheek): **OK, the goal here is to see how long you can hang on to your worries. But the other helpful people in our group are going to try to help you get rid of them.** Give a signal and let group members try to step on and pop the other balloons while keeping their own out of reach. People can continue to play even after their own balloons have popped, so it doesn't usually take long for all of the balloons to become memories. *Then* you can throw away the lists along with the popped balloons.

Step 2

Before you do anything else in this step, let group members brainstorm the things they are currently worried about. Then ask them to agree on "weights" for each worry, ranging from one pound to one hundred pounds. (If they can't reach an agreement, take an average.) One of the advantages of a small group is that it becomes easier to direct your teaching toward group members' specific needs. So the better you can determine those needs, the more effective you can be in supplying examples and valuable help during the rest of the session.

Step 3

It won't take the members of a small group long to find their individual places on the continuum, so let everyone have some experience in being both Sluggards and Worriers. Establish a signal that you can give that will clue the group to switch from one extreme to the other. Begin as a group of Sluggards as you ask questions and generate group discussion. (**Do you think the Bulls will win the championship this year? How do you like school? What's the best thing that's happened to you this week? What's the worst?**) As soon as group members begin to get into a rhythm, sound the signal and have them immediately switch to Worriers. When they've had some practice, sound the signal more and more often. Then you can put up the continuum and see where the kids think they belong.

Step 2

Begin this step by having group members, one person at a time, share personal worries. Challenge them to share worries that they think no one else in the room will have. (You might first rattle off a list of common worries: grades, dating relationships, getting into college, not being liked by others, and so forth.) In a large group, it's good to let members maintain their individuality from time to time. In addition, this is an excellent way to get to know each other better. For example, you might discover that one person is anxiously awaiting word on a scholarship, that someone has a seriously ill relative, that someone is hoping to get into medical school, and so forth. Keep going around until group members cannot think of anything else. But once kids get started in thinking of specific concerns, they usually get better at it.

Step 4

When you get to the point in the discussion in which students consider what they might want to do over the summer, divide into teams and let your group members make the points made by the author. Form three teams: (1) summer fun and recreation; (2) saving money for college, a car, etc.; and (3) participating in a mission or service project. Each team should explore the possibilities of its assigned activity from three perspectives— (1) a Sluggard; (2) a Worrier; and (3) someone who trusts God for wisdom and help. In other words, each team will report on three courses of action for its assigned area of concern. The teams should discover that attitudes can make significant differences in the results of any decision. They should also arrive, by their own logic and common sense, at a good balance between worry and inaction.

Step 2

Instead of using Repro Resource 4, create a list of worries and let kids rate them in significance using a scale of 1 (least) to 10 (most). Kids can vote simply by holding up the number of fingers they feel is appropriate. Here are some worries you might use:

• **A mom sees her two year old tottering on the edge of a cliff.**

• **Your mom might fix Spam omelets for breakfast tomorrow.**

• **It looks like you're going to make a D in English this term.**

• **Your parents are fighting a lot, and it sounds serious.**

Afterward, read aloud Matthew 6:25-34. Then ask: **How in the world could Jesus tell us not to worry? Don't people have every right to show concern over most of the things we listed?** See if anyone makes a distinction between worry and concern. Eventually kids should discover that concern for others is a basic element of Christian love. What Jesus refers to, however, is worry about things we can't control.

Step 4

Try to deal with Steps 3 and 4 together. Begin by comparing the Matthew 6 and Proverbs 6 passages. Before putting up the continuum or getting into the text material, try to generate some challenging questions that will spark debate among your group members. For instance, you might ask: **If Jesus commanded us not to worry in one place, how can we possibly be expected to model our lives after the ant, who works like crazy all of the time? If it's the pagans who "run after" things they want, isn't that what we will appear to be if we become ant-like workers trying to provide for our own needs?** See if group members can make appropriate distinctions between worry and apathy, genuine work and being "driven" to make money due to a lack of faith in God's provision, etc.

Step 2

Using Repro Resource 2 is a good way to get new people involved with Scripture. For those who don't know the Bible very well, you might want to follow up with an explanation of the context of the Sermon on the Mount, from which this passage comes. Point out that Jesus was making some bold challenges as to how people related to each other and to God. He was not satisfied with "status quo," and was instead providing a much higher level of expectation (and satisfaction with life). Encourage questions about the Bible text. If kids don't ask anything, *you* should. To make sure they understand what is being said, ask: **Is it realistic for people to not worry about anything? What's so wrong with being concerned for food, shelter, clothing, and the other basics in life? Why would Jesus say something like this—doesn't He care about us?** Make sure kids understand that the only way we can do as Jesus instructs is to strengthen our relationship with Him, which is always beneficial to us.

Step 3

Begin this step with a review of Jesus's statement in Matthew 6:27. Ask: **If you knew you had only one more hour to live, how would you spend it? Do you think you would enjoy that hour?** Some might attempt a lot of thrilling (death-defying) activities, but more than likely, it would be impossible for us to enjoy anything if we knew we were about to die. The only worthwhile activities would seem to be anything that would bring us closer to God. Explain that Jesus was making essentially the same point. We can spend our lives doing any variety of activities, but anything that takes us away from God usually involves a great deal of worry. And how much can we truly enjoy anything we worry about? So it is much more beneficial to include God in all of our needs—physical and emotional, as well as spiritual—and use our energies in getting to know Him better rather than worrying.

Step 2

Have someone read aloud Matthew 6:25-34 as if the words were being spoken by Jesus on the mountainside. All other group members should listen as if they were hearing the words for the first time. After the reading, ask: **What questions would you have? What was said here that might make you feel good? Did anything that was said make you feel a bit of confusion or hesitation?** Encourage group members to be completely honest about their feelings. Then spend some time dealing with any possible misunderstandings or negative feelings. Finally, have group members share their current worries. Explain that the rest of the session will deal with helping each person keep a proper perspective on his or her worries. But to make it more effective, group members should become vulnerable to each other about the things they are feeling and/or worrying about.

Step 5

It's easy to say, "Don't worry. Trust God." Most kids will truly believe that is the correct thing to do. However, we all experience pressures that cause us to get off track from time to time. So at the end of the session, work together as a group to write a prayer to be used whenever personal worries become stronger than they should. It need not be long or complicated, but it should be complete. Ask: **When we begin to get worried, what things do we need to confess to God? What requests do we need to make of Him? What steps do we need to take?** When your group completes a prayer that everyone is satisfied with, arrange to have copies made and distributed at the next meeting.

Step 1

After completing the blindfold activity and reading Matthew 6:34, ask group members to decide how they would feel if they *could* know everything about the future. Ask: **What difference would this make? Do you think you would worry less? Why or why not?**

Step 3

Have your group members form two teams for a debate. Ask the teams to prepare their responses to the following statement, assigning a yes response to one team and a no to the other: "Spending a lot of time planning what to wear and how to look attractive is inappropriate worry." After the teams have had some planning time, allow them to present their arguments.

Step 2

To begin this step, ask: **What are your weaknesses?** Guys may be slow to respond at first. (After all, they're *guys*.) But go on to explain that even Superman was susceptible to Kryptonite. Indiana Jones had a terrible fear of snakes. Samson was rendered powerless by a haircut. Explain that there is no shame in admitting our weaknesses. In fact, there is more danger in denying that we are affected by certain things. After guys begin to open up a bit, turn the discussion toward worry. It might be that these potential weaknesses are sources of worry for your group of guys. Ask: **To what degree do you worry about these things? How can you tell when you begin to worry about something?** After group members respond, keep their specific questions and comments in mind as you move ahead with the session.

Step 4

At an appropriate spot during this step, ask: **What are some "manly" things that guys do to keep from showing that they're worried about something? What macho things do they do to cope with worry?** Some guys may admit to withdrawing from friends and/or family members and dealing with the problem in silence. Some may get angry or violent (even to the point of hitting something) as a response. Some may go jogging or work out, counting on the sweat and fatigue to lessen the concerns they feel. Sometimes, if guys are worried that they can't do something, they will take a stupid dare to prove that they can. Explain that as they get older, men who mishandle worry frequently have workaholic tendencies as well as higher probabilities of ulcers, heart attacks, and other health problems. Challenge your group of guys to learn *now* to deal with worry in productive ways, rather than expecting to do something about it later.

Step 2

Play a game of "You Think *You're* Worried?" Have kids sit in a circle. The first person says, "You think *you're* worried? *I'm* worried about _____." The second person repeats the phrase and the first person's worry, and then adds a worry of his or her own. The third person must repeat the first two worries and add a new one. (You get the idea.) Truthful answers may show through in spots, but encourage kids to have fun with this exercise. So by the time the sixth person has a turn, he or she might say, "You think you're worried? I'm worried about going to school in my pajamas one day, dying from eating bad liver, having to work at Burger Buddy my whole life, discovering that my future wife grows fangs during full moons, forgetting the quadratic equation after I graduate, and beginning to wear pants like my dad when I get to be his age." Whenever someone is unable to remember all of the previous comments, he or she is out and the game continues. Play until one person remains.

Step 3

Rather than merely discuss the differences between sluggards and worriers, roleplay a world that consists of only these two personality types. Divide into two groups. Designate one group as cheerleaders for the Sluggard High School Slugs. Designate the other group as cheerleaders for Worry High School Warts. Explain that an imaginary game is taking place. Have the cheerleaders create some cheers appropriate for its school. In addition, you can play the role of stadium announcer, and the cheerleading groups can react to your announcements. For example, you might announce at intervals:

• **Please rise to sing the national anthem.**

• **It looks like a player is hurt.**

• **That's the end of the first half. Worry High is ahead 36-0.**

• **A fight has broken out on the field.**

MEDIA

Step 3

As you discuss Sluggards and Worriers, ask group members to think of TV and movie characters who fit these descriptions. When they think of someone, kids should stand and do an impromptu impersonation while others guess who it is. If you wish, you might also be ready to show some of your favorite scenes of classic worriers (Woody Allen, Barney Fife, etc.) or sluggards (Fred Sanford, Al Bundy, Homer Simpson, etc.). But count on kids to come up with the characters who are most relevant to them. Use their characters as examples as you continue the session.

Step 5

Conclude your session by playing the Bobby McFerrin song, "Don't Worry, Be Happy" (from the album *Simple Pleasures,* © 1988, EMI-Manhattan Records). The song consists of simple rhyming couplets followed by the phrase, "Don't worry, be happy." It is a simple matter to create additional verses to incorporate the things group members have learned. Play the song to provide the meter and rhythm as students work on their own verses. You may want to have them work in teams so your more creative people can help others. When everyone has come up with one or two verses, perform your version of the song by going from person to person (or team to team) to hear group members sing what they've written. Everyone should join in on the "Don't worry, be happy" part each time. Afterward, discuss how the message of this song is similar to or different from Jesus' teaching on worry.

SHORT MEETING TIME

Step 1

Open the session by having everyone create his or her own "Top Ten List" of things he or she worries about. Explain that according to statistics, less than ten percent of the things we worry about ever come to pass. So in most cases, group members need be concerned about only one of the things on their lists. Then spend time reading and discussing Matthew 6:25-34 to see what Jesus recommends for handling the remaining items on their lists. Use portions of Step 2 where applicable. And since the kids have already made their lists, the exercise in Step 5 (determining which things they need to take action on and which ones to let go of) is good to use to conclude the meeting.

Step 2

Open the session with Step 2 (beginning with Repro Resource 4), and cover the material thoroughly. Ask kids to provide their own specific examples as they go along. (When the topic is worry, kids should have no trouble coming up with examples.) Encourage questions and comments along the way, and personalize the session as much as possible. Then, if time permits, move on to Step 5. If not, summarize the key points of your discussion and close in prayer.

URBAN

Step 3

On the board, draw two gauge-looking devices (that look like speedometers). Label one of them "Worry Meter"; label the other "Sluggard Meter." Draw three zones of intensity on each meter: "Low," "Medium," and "High." On the "Worry Meter" these zones will represent the amount of *trust* in God group members will need to reduce worry. On the "Sluggard Meter," the zones will represent the amount of *self-motivation* group members will need to reduce their sluggardly ways. Have each group member ponder where he or she believes he or she is on each meter. Then distribute paper and pencils. Instruct each group member to write a plan for increasing trust and self-motivation in each of the following six areas:
(1) personal life
(2) family life
(3) relationships with others
(4) prayer (faith) life
(5) at school
(6) in the city

Step 4

Have your group members discuss what they'd say to the following people:
• a woman who's afraid to leave her home for fear of being mugged or raped.
• a person who's having sex with a lot of different partners and isn't at all worried about AIDS.
• a person on welfare who has the ability to work, but not the interest.

You could also have kids roleplay conversations with these people or write an advice column directed to them.

Step 1

For some reason, junior highers seem to have a particular affinity for *Mad* magazine. Find a recent issue or two that features Alfred E. Newman prominently on the cover. (It shouldn't be hard, since most of them do.) Hold up the issue(s) and ask: **How much do you know about this guy?** Let students respond. Then say (tongue in cheek): **Mr. Newman is also a model of a mature Christian. He demonstrates one essential quality that Jesus taught us to exhibit.** Encourage group members to speculate about what you might be talking about. If no one figures it out, remind them that Alfred E. Newman's motto is, "What, me worry?" Explain that the topic of today's session is how to keep from needless worry. Later, when you get to the definition of a sluggard, you can again hold up the covers and clarify that even though Alfred E. Newman manages to avoid worry, perhaps his method is not the best one.

Step 4

If you have a lot of junior highers, you'll probably want to change the "How might you spend your summer?" anecdote in this step. Most junior highers don't yet devote a lot of time to worrying about college, cars, summer jobs, and so forth. Perhaps, instead, you could let them envision the summer between junior high and high school as they consider specifics of Worriers vs. Sluggards. What might they be worrying about? (Losing old friends; not being accepted; too much change and challenge; etc.) How might their sluggard tendencies take over? (Keeping to themselves rather than making the most of the time with their current friends; refusing to read books or otherwise start preparing for a more disciplined schedule; etc.) Make sure to keep the discussion at an applicable level for your younger students.

Step 2

After you discuss Jesus' teaching about worry, challenge kids to come up with specific examples. Ask each person to try to think of a Bible character and circumstance in which the person's faith defeated worry. (If your kids aren't up to this challenge, form teams and let each team brainstorm ideas.) You might want to award some kind of "extra credit" for kids who can also provide the proper Scripure reference for the stories they think of. If you wish, you can compile their answers, make copies for everyone, and hand them out at a future meeting.

Step 5

Ask: **When we stop worrying, does that mean bad things will stop happening to us? If not, what might we assume Jesus is trying to tell us when He says not to worry so much?** As students think about the life of Jesus, they may discover that He never seemed to worry. Yet His life ended in the greatest possible degree of unfairness, suffering, and pain. Perhaps Jesus wants us to discover that constant worrying is worse than occasional suffering. The sooner we learn to expect a certain amount of injustice, persecution, and discomfort, the better off we can be. We're going to have our share of those things whether or not we worry about them. So if we can learn to stop worrying, even while anticipating occasional periods of unpleasantness, we'll be better off. You might want to discuss Paul's notation of this discovery. "I have learned to be content whatever the circumstances. I know what it is to be in need, and I know what it is to have plenty. I have learned the secret of being content in any and every situation, whether well fed or hungry, whether living in plenty or in want. I can do everything through Him who gives me strength" (Philippians 4:11-13). Follow with a prayer that God will provide the strength for your group members to remain faithful to Him and worry-free, no matter what their circumstances.

Date Used: 03/19

Approx. Time

Step 1: The Blindfold Conspiracy _____
o Extra Action
o Mostly Girls
o Short Meeting Time
o Combined Junior High/High School
Things needed: *blind folds - 3/4*

Step 2: Why Worry Shouldn't Win _____
o Small Group
☑ Large Group
☑ Heard It All Before
o Little Bible Background
o Fellowship & Worship
o Mostly Guys
o Extra Fun
o Short Meeting Time
o Extra Challenge
Things needed:

Step 3: Extreme Thinking _____
o Small Group
o Little Bible Background
o Mostly Girls
o Extra Fun
o Media
o Urban
Things needed:

Step 4: Getting Concrete _____
o Large Group
o Heard It All Before
o Mostly Guys
o Urban
o Combined Junior High/High School
Things needed:

Step 5: Walking Away from Worry _____
o Extra Action
o Fellowship & Worship
o Media
o Extra Challenge
Things needed:

Why Bother with Annoying People?

YOUR GOALS FOR THIS SESSION:

C h o o s e   o n e   o r   m o r e

☐ To help kids discover what it means to love enemies in the biblical sense.

☐ To help kids understand that they can work through anger and resentment toward enemies without putting their enemies down or being unkind to them.

☐ To help kids choose to pray for enemies in specific ways.

☐ Other _____
_____

Your Bible Base:

Matthew 5:43-45
I Corinthians 13:4-7
II Corinthians 11:20
Ephesians 4:26

People You Love to Hate

(Needed: Paper, pencils, prizes)

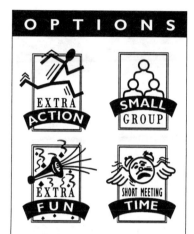

Distribute paper and pencils. Instruct group members to write the numbers 1-5 on their papers. Emphasize that there should be no talking during the following activity.

Then ask: **What are your five biggest pet peeves—the five things that irritate you most? List them from one to five on your paper.**

Wait for your group members to finish their lists. Then, when you say **Go,** group members should go around the room and try to find other people who share the same pet peeves. When a person finds someone who has a peeve he or she listed, the two should initial each other's papers next to that item. (The wording does not have to be exact, obviously, but the peeves should be similar. You'll be the judge in case of close calls.) The first person to get all five peeves initialed (or the most peeves initialed after a certain amount of time) is the winner.

Award a prize to the winner. You may also want to award a prize to the two people whose lists were most similar and to the person whose pet peeves were unique (the person with the least number of signatures).

Ask: **How do you feel about people who exhibit these pet peeves or who do things that irritate you?** Get responses from several group members. If no one mentions it, suggest that people who irritate us regularly can become our enemies. That's the topic of this session—dealing with enemies.

Combat Styles

(Needed: Scrap paper, pencils, copies of Repro Resource 5)

Ask: **What is an enemy?** (Someone who doesn't want to be friendly with you; someone you feel suspicious of or competitive with; someone whose values are so different from yours that he or she threatens you; someone who is difficult to deal with or who has hurt you; etc.)

Explain: **By these definitions, an enemy could be a teacher, coach, or parent, as well as people at school who bug you or are out to get you. There are times when even brothers and sisters or friends can become our enemies.**

Distribute pieces of scrap paper. Instruct group members to write down the names of people they would define as enemies. Emphasize that no one else will see what they write down.

Say: **You don't have to answer this question out loud, but look at the names you wrote down. How do you usually deal with these people?** Give group members a moment to consider the question.

Distribute copies of "If You Were on the Yellow Brick Road" (Repro Resource 5). Give group members a minute or two to choose their answers. Then ask each person to tell the group which character he or she selected and why.

Afterward, say: **These are four ways that people commonly respond to an enemy. They are what we consider normal behavior. That's why one of the toughest passages in the Bible is Matthew 5:43-45.** Ask a volunteer to read the passage aloud.

Then ask: **How does Jesus say Christians should treat their enemies?** (We should love them and pray for them.)

Point out (or allow group members to point out) that it's not natural for us to love our enemies or pray for them. Then, before you go on, ask group members if there's anything unusual that stands out to them in this passage. They might notice, for instance, that Jesus says by loving our enemies we are being like God Himself. That's what makes this teaching so radical. You will come back to this idea later in the session.

O P T I O N S

LITTLE BIBLE BACKGROUND

FELLOWSHIP & WORSHIP

MOSTLY GUYS

MEDIA

SHORT MEETING TIME

JR. HIGH / HIGH SCHOOL COMBINED

EXTRA CHALLENGE

Love in Enemy Territory

(Needed: Copies of Repro Resource 6, Bibles, pencils)

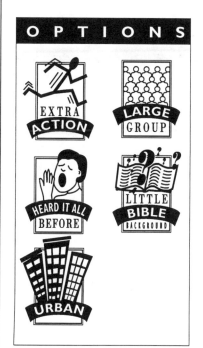

Distribute copies of "Love Is . . ." (Repro Resource 6). Say: **Part of what makes it difficult to love our enemies is that we aren't sure what "love" is and isn't. Let's look at I Corinthians 13:4-7 and see how it helps us define love.** Ask a volunteer read the passage aloud. Then, as a group, go over the instructions for Repro Resource 6.

Have group members work in pairs in completing the worksheet. When they're finished, have each pair share its responses. Use the following answers to supplement group members' responses.

(1) Yes. Love does not boast, it is not proud (I Corinthians 13:4).

(2) No. "Always trusts" (13:7) doesn't mean we have to trust our enemies to keep our secrets. It means that we trust them enough that we aren't always suspicious of them.

(3) No. It would be phony to pretend to enjoy being with them. But we can be polite and kind (13:4, 5).

(4) Yes. Love "is kind" (13:4) and "rejoices with the truth" (13:6), but "is not rude" (13:5). Mudslinging, or telling others how terrible someone is, is "delight[ing] in evil" (13:6). It can be tough to speak the truth, and it can be tough to speak with love, but we are commanded to do both (Ephesians 4:15).

(5) Yes. "Love does not delight in evil" (I Corinthians 13:6). We may see that they've gotten what they deserve, but we shouldn't see it as personal revenge.

(6) Yes. "Love is patient" (13:4), "[love] always hopes," and "always perseveres" (13:7) means that we're willing to give people the benefit of the doubt. "Keeps no record of wrongs" (13:5) means we should be willing to forgive and start again.

(7) Yes. If we keep no record of wrongs, we aren't concerned about getting even. Being "kind" (13:4) is the opposite of getting even.

(8) No. While we don't need to be defensive, we can stand up for ourselves. Justice is a concern for Christians; therefore, we "[speak] the truth in love" (Ephesians 4:15).

(9) Yes. Love is kind, it does not boast, it is not rude or self-seeking (I Corinthians 13:4, 5). Putting someone down is usually a form of lifting yourself up.

(10) No. Love does not mean we condone wrongdoing. "Love does

not delight in evil but rejoices with the truth" (13:6).

Have someone read aloud II Corinthians 11:20. Explain that in this passage, Paul is rebuking the Corinthians for following abusive, authoritarian false teachers instead of the true apostle (himself), who came to them humbly and never demanded anything from them. In this passage it is clear that Paul does not advocate Christians letting themselves be abused or exploited—at least not by people who claimed to be preachers and teachers.

Ask: **So what is the difference? How do we truly love our enemies without becoming victims of abuse or exploitation?** Get several responses.

Then have group members consider the example Jesus gave. Ask: **Did Jesus allow Himself to be taken advantage of on the cross?** (Some group members may say yes. After all, Jesus let Himself be whipped, beaten, scorned, and crucified—and He never defended Himself. He never even opened His mouth. Other group members may say no. After all, in reality, Jesus was in charge every step of the way. His persecution was a master plan to pay for the sins of the world. He chose not to defend Himself or to stop even His own murder, though the Bible says He could have called 72,000 angels to deliver Him if had chosen to [Matthew 26:53].)

STEP
4

What Love Looks Like

Ask two volunteers to participate in a couple of spontaneous roleplays. One of the volunteers will be play a kid who's attempting to love his or her enemies. The other volunteer will play his or her enemy.

Have the two actors sit next to each other in front of the group. Explain that the actors will perform each roleplay twice. In the first roleplay, your actors will demonstrate what happens when the first doesn't do well in "loving" his or her enemy. In the second roleplay, the actors will demonstrate what happens when the first person does well in loving his or her enemy.

The situation in the first roleplay is that the enemy is making fun of the other person's shoes. The situation in the second roleplay is that the enemy is bragging about having just received a new car from his or her parents. Allow each roleplay to run about 45-60 seconds.

After each roleplay has been performed twice, ask the rest of your

group members to evaluate the first person's performance in loving his or her enemy. Did he or she do a good job? What else could he or she have done?

Afterward, give your actors a round of applause. Then say: **Sometimes it's easier to "love" an enemy when you're face-to-face with him or her than it is to love him or her when you're with others. For instance, have you ever been in a group in which someone started gossiping or talking badly about someone you didn't like?** (Probably most of your group members have.)

What's the temptation in a situation like that? (To join in the gossiping.)

What *should* we do in a situation like that? (Say nothing at all, change the topic of conversation, defend the person being talked about, etc.)

What if you feel really angry at your enemy? Should you pretend that you aren't? Get responses from several group members. Then have someone read aloud Ephesians 4:26.

Explain: **The sin isn't anger—it's holding a grudge or seeking revenge. What are some practical things you can do to avoid sinning in your anger?** Use the following suggestions to supplement group members' responses.

• The ideal solution is to talk with the person one-on-one about the problem. However, that's not always possible.

• If you're really upset and talking to the person is impossible or doesn't help, journaling is an excellent tool for venting your feelings. Write down your feelings and ask God to help you deal with them.

• It can also be helpful to find someone else to talk to about your feelings. But be careful that you don't just rag on your enemy or get the other person to side with you against your enemy. Choose someone who will understand how you feel and be supportive of you, but who will also challenge you as well. So much the better if this person can act as mediator between you and your enemy.

Prayer Conquers All

Wrap up your session on loving our enemies with the following comments: **When Jesus told us to love our enemies, He knew a tremendous secret: You can't hate someone if you really pray for that person. You can still hate what the person does, but you can't hate him or her. Let's list some things we could pray for our enemies.** Use the following ideas to supplement group members' responses.

• Pray for reconciliation with the person if it's a broken friendship or family relationship.

• Pray that the person would come to know Christ or that his or her relationship with Christ would grow.

• Pray for the person's physical, emotional, or spiritual health. (Sometimes illness or chronic pain can make a person grouchy and affect his or her behavior.)

• Pray for Christ to form His character in his or her life *and* in yours.

• Pray that God would help the person work through insecure feelings. (Teachers facing retirement can be fearful and grouchy; parents who don't know how to handle kids can overreact; kids who hate themselves hate everyone else too; etc.)

Close the session by praying for your group members' enemies. Include some of the preceding issues in your prayer.

After the session, make yourself available to talk privately to group members who are dealing with serious situations. For instance, when someone we love—such as a parent—is abusive, it's very hard to follow the advice given in this session. Be available to pray with these kids and walk with them through their difficult situations.

If You Were on the —·—··—··—

Yellow Brick Road

In dealing with your enemies, which of the following characters from *The Wizard of Oz* do you act most like?

Scarecrow

"Usually I can't outwit my enemies. I don't have the brains to come up with terrible things to say to them when they tease me—but I wish I did. I usually just keep my anger bottled up inside me."

Tin Man

"I don't really have a heart for my enemies, but I pretend I do. I usually try to be nice to my enemies so they won't get mad at me."

Cowardly Lion

"I don't have the courage to face my enemies. If I see one in the convenience store after school, I'll go somewhere else."

Wicked Witch of the West

"I'm mean to my enemies. I treat them badly and they hate me. In fact, some of them are scared of me."

Read each of the following statements. If the statement describes something that's involved in loving enemies, write "Yes" in the blank. Then write the phrase from I Corinthians 13:4-7 or Ephesians 4:26 that the statement illustrates. (The first one is done for you this way.) If the statement does *not* describe something that's involved in loving enemies, write "No" in the blank.

Loving my enemies means I should ...

(1) avoid bragging about myself and competing with them.

Yes. Love does not boast, it is not proud (I Corinthians 13:4).

(2) try to be best friends with them and tell them all my secrets.

_____

(3) pretend that I enjoy being with them.

_____

(4) speak the truth in a kind but matter-of-fact way, without gossiping or being a mudslinger.

_____

(5) not be glad when bad things happen to them.

_____

(6) be ready to forgive them.

_____

(7) not try to get even with them.

_____

(8) let them take advantage of me.

_____

(9) avoid putting them down (in words and tone of voice).

_____

(10) pretend that I like their wrong behavior or that I approve of it.

_____

Step 1

Rather than having each person write out his or her pet peeves, start out with kids in teams. Instruct each team to discuss the pet peeves of each of its individual members, compile a list, agree on an order of irritation (from most irritating to least irritating), and be ready to act out the situations it has listed. Then have each team perform the top item on its list. (Performances need not be long or complicated. Most pet peeves can be demonstrated in just a few seconds.) When teams finish acting out their situations, have them explain exactly what pet peeve they were trying to communicate. See how many other teams listed the same (or a very similar) pet peeve. Teams need not duplicate something that has already been acted out. They should instead go on to the next item on their lists.

Step 3

Using the behaviors listed on Repro Resource 6, create conflict situations between two people and deal with them as court cases. For example, the behavior for #2 could become "The Case of the Secretive, So-called Friend," in which Joe Smith accuses Jane Jones of not being a true friend because she won't pass along information she knows about some third party. (Tailor the specifics to fit your own group.) Appoint a judge, prosecutor, defender, and defendant in each case. The other students become jury members. (Jury members don't have to just sit there. They can ask questions "for clarification" of the prosecutor, defender, or judge.) You'll probably need to choose which of the "cases" you want to act out. Students can then take home the handout to deal with the others on their own.

Step 1

In a small group, trying to match pet peeves from a five-item list is not likely to be as effective or feasible as in a large group. So instead have kids form pairs and come up with as many pet peeves as they can think of. They should brainstorm for quantity, rather than quality at first. As pairs report on what they've come up with, record all of their responses in a master list on the board. Afterward, let each person "vote" for his or her top five choices as you tally the votes on the side. Then you can easily see the vote total and determine which are the most annoying pet peeves for your group as a whole.

Step 4

The roleplays in this step call for a few volunteers, but in a small group try to get everyone involved. The roleplays set up conflict situations between individuals, but they can be just as effective between two groups of friends who don't get along with each other. In fact, peer influence may be a major reason why some of your group members don't settle disagreements with their "enemies" more quickly. So add some "supporting players" to the roleplays as written and have all group members take part. Later, discuss not only the feelings of the people directly involved in the conflict, but the attitudes and actions of their friends as well.

Step 3

Make two copies of Repro Resource 6 for each person. The first time through, ask group members to ignore the instructions. Have kids fill out the sheet based on their actual actions and attitudes—not according to what the correct biblical answers would be. As stated, #1 on the sheet reads, "Loving my enemies means I should avoid bragging about myself and competing with them." But revise it to read, "If loving my enemies means I avoid bragging about myself and competing with them . . ." Students should then finish the statement with either "I love my enemies" or "I guess I don't love my enemies." The advantage of doing this in a large group is that when kids complete their sheets, you can review their answers, figure the percentage of people who answered each way, and determine approximately how loving your group is from a statistical standpoint. You will also be able to see which specific areas are strongest and weakest in your group. Then you can hand out the second copy of Repro Resource 6, have group members do the assignment as written, and discover what kinds of goals they should set for themselves.

Step 4

Rather than having just a couple of people involved in the roleplays as written, divide into teams and have each team create a conflict skit based on the personal experiences of one of its members. Some skits may reflect good conflict resolution on the part of the people involved. Others probably won't. In either case, skits shouldn't deviate too much from what actually happened. After each team performs its skit, the other group members should comment on how the conflict was handled. What actions do they agree with? What things might they have done differently? (These real-life conflict situations can also be used as specific examples when you deal with conflict resolution later in the session.)

Step 3

As important as I Corinthians 13 is to our understanding of what real love should be, this is a section of Scripture that probably triggers the "heard it all before" reflex quicker than almost any other. You still need to have kids deal with it, but you may not want to use Repro Resource 6 if they think they already know it. Instead, have them read the chapter and create a profile of the world's *least* loving person. Rather than letting them get by with "He's quick to become angry, not patient, not kind," challenge them to come up with specific actions that would reflect such characteristics. Use the example of Paul Bunyan or Pecos Bill, and explain that this person should become another legend of folklore based on his or her unloving behavior. After they've written a paragraph or two, have group members share their profiles. Then point out that no one could possibly be as bad as the characters who have been described. Thankfully, everyone has some good qualities, and we should focus on those traits as we try to love our enemies.

Step 4

Create a dispute between two groups of people that might require a negotiator to help settle it. (Most kids probably won't relate well to negotiating peace treaties, labor contracts, or other "adult" situations. Some of them might be better acquainted with gang treaties or perhaps marriage/ divorce counseling.) Let a person who may assume he or she knows it all already be the negotiator. Everyone else should take a side and try to hold firm to his or her position. See how well the negotiator does with a lot of intense feeling on both sides of the dispute. It's one thing to discuss the importance of reconciliation; it's something else to know how to practice it effectively. After the roleplay, point out that we may not be able to influence the actions and attitudes of other people, but we are certainly responsible for our own. We can learn to "negotiate" conflicts that may involve some of our own selfish behaviors.

Step 2

Begin this step by having group members complete some sentences. Start with **"I hate . . ."**; move on to **"I hate it when . . ."**; and conclude with **"I hate people who . . ."** See how long it takes for personal conflicts to be mentioned. The first two sentences might focus on detested foods, classes, or situations. But they might also include barriers between the speaker and certain types of people. If not, those are likely to come out in response to the third sentence. Discuss how comfortably most of us are able to speak of "hate"—perhaps for no good reason. Then continue with Step 2, emphasizing Jesus' command to love our enemies. Ask: **Is this possible? Is it feasible? Is it really important not to hate anyone? Why?** If you raise more questions than answers at this point, that's fine. Many of the questions will be answered during the rest of the session.

Step 3

If your group is new to the basic teachings of the Bible, I Corinthians 13 is an excellent place to let them linger for a while. When you get to Repro Resource 6, make sure not to rush them. Give them plenty of time to come up with their answers. Also take your time as you discuss the handout and add comments as noted in the session text. Encourage questions about any of the statements on the Repro Resource. While the Bible text is clear and easy to understand, the applications may seem unnatural and confusing. (If so, explain that the applications aren't natural—they're *supernatural*. Only God can provide the degree of love described in this passage. We fall far short when we rely on our own efforts.) If this is a new passage to your group members, encourage them to reread it every night during the next week. Each reading is likely to initiate new insights into God's love and how we should apply it toward each other.

Step 2

Ask each group member to share briefly about one personal experience with an enemy. (But emphasize that kids shouldn't mention any names.) After each group member shares, briefly discuss how the person became an enemy and how the group member feels about that person today. Has anyone's Christian faith made a difference in the relationship? Be prepared to share a story of your own, preferably one in which there was reconciliation with the enemy.

Step 5

This session concludes with a natural worship activity—detailed prayer for those people we might consider our enemies. Yet the tendency for some group members may be to pray (and truly mean it), but then leave the session and not give the matter any more thought. Remind group members that a genuine love for God is proven by our actions toward each other (1 John 4:19-21). Consequently, their worship will not be complete by simply praying and leaving. Therefore, also ask each person to think of one "action step" that would initiate reconciliation with one of his or her "enemies." This step might include sending an anonymous card or gift, offering to do something together, making an apology for a past action, etc. Then include in your closing prayer a request for God to provide the courage for each person to take his or her predetermined step sometime during the following week, and for His help in achieving reconciliation in each person's relationship.

Step 4

In addition to the roleplay situations described in the session, ask your group members to think of two or three other situations that might arise with an enemy. Using these situations, have your volunteers present each one twice. The first presentation should detail a poor attempt at "loving" the enemy; the second should detail a more successful attempt. As you talk about the situations, discuss the role competition plays in creating a difficult relationship. Ask: **Can people become enemies because of natural competition? What are we usually competitive about? When can understanding our own competitive natures help us with those we don't get along with?**

Step 5

After listing the ideas about praying for our enemies, talk about the times in which we aren't willing to pray for them. Ask: **What do you do when you can't pray for the person who has hurt you? Are you willing to let that person come between you and God because you don't want to talk to God about him or her? Even if it isn't easy to pray, can you admit to yourself that God loves that person as much as He loves you? How does acknowledging that God loves that person affect your thinking?**

Step 2

Most guys won't need a lot of help understanding how enemy relationships get formed. Many of them are likely to have been in fights—or intense ongoing arguments—with other guys. For some of them, conflict may be a fine art. To see how good your group is at starting conflicts, randomly select two volunteers. The first person should try to initiate a fight with the second one. The second person should react as he would normally. Other observers should note the techniques of how conflicts get started (name-calling, cruel teasing, physical abuse, etc.). They should also decide whether the second person was justified in his response, and suggest actions he might have taken instead. Afterward, point out that Jesus wasn't just talking to women when He said we should love our enemies.

Step 4

With a group of guys, you may want to spend more time discussing how to handle anger. The advice given in the session (talk one-on-one, write in a journal, or talk to someone else) is good, but guys may need more options. Begin by having them make a list of things they've tried that haven't worked well—things *not* to do when you get angry. (Guys may have stories of hitting trees, kicking immovable objects, etc.) While some reactions may be comical, don't miss the serious problem of being unable to control anger. Guys who are physically bigger and stronger than other people need outlets for anger that don't involve violence. Brainstorm what some of those outlets might be. (You might suggest going for a long run to work off energy, playing a sport in which you can take out your anger on a ball, or finding a place in which you can be alone until your anger subsides.) Everyone should come up with at least three options that he feels would work for him. Challenge group members to remember these options the next time they get angry.

Step 1

Open the session with a group-participation skit titled, "A World without Conflict." The setting should be someplace where young people tend to congregate, such as a mall or school cafeteria. As kids meet and interact, explain that they are to remain happy and sweet—no matter what is said or done to them. Then add that, of course, there may be *some* people in the crowd who will take advantage of this situation and say exactly what they think of others. Have kids mill around (in character) and converse. Some of them are certain to "test the waters" and see if they can provoke conflict. Watch to see how others handle such attempts. Do they smile through gritted teeth? Do they break down and react negatively? Do they come right back with equally nasty comments without shifting out of their pleasant demeanor? Afterward, discuss the activity. Point out that a world without conflict seems phony and unrealistic. We live in the "real" world—one filled with conflict, misunderstanding, and personality clashes. We are certain to form enemies as we interact with other people, so we need to know what to do in such cases.

Step 5

Close the session by playing "Hug Tag." You'll need an odd number of people to play. Everyone should have a partner, except for one person who is "It." Explain that everyone should hug his or her partner until you give a signal. Then kids should let go and wander around the room. When you give a second signal, they must again find a partner—but not the one they had previously. When two people are hugging, they are safe. In the meantime, as soon as you give the second signal, "It" will be trying to find a partner, which will leave someone else partnerless. That person then becomes "It." After a while, shift from hug partners to hug trios or quartets. Afterward, point out that hugging to bond together is a lot more fun than holding grudges and making enemies.

Step 2

After discussing the conflict-management styles of the *Wizard of Oz* characters, say: **You know, someone has done a "Christian version" of Mother Goose as well as other classic works of literature. But no one has done *The Wizard of Oz* yet. Maybe we should.** Show one of your favorite scenes from the film on video and then ask volunteers to reenact the scene as it might be done in a Christian version. Depending on what your group members think about products such as the "Christian Mother Goose," you may get a serious treatment of the scene or a whimsical parody. But either way, group members will probably come up with some significant observations and applications that apply to Christian behavior as we relate to people who are different than we are—the people we may classify as enemies.

Step 5

To close the session and to help group members see where some of their conflict-management skills may have originated, show some classic cartoons. Try to choose some that emphasize an ongoing adversarial relationship between the characters (Elmer Fudd and Bugs Bunny, Sylvester and Tweety Bird, or even a few Itchy and Scratchy segments from *The Simpsons* [which are hard-hitting parodies of the violent nature of some cartoon shows]). Ask volunteers to tell what their favorite cartoons were as children, and what they learned about conflict from those shows. If possible, you might want to conclude with a Road Runner cartoon. Explain that he is an excellent model. By ignoring and/or outsmarting Wile E. Coyote, rather than trying to retaliate, Road Runner's perpetual enemy almost always does himself in. We can learn much from that example.

Step 1

Open the session with a word-association game. Have each person in turn provide a different synonym for the word *enemy*. Whenever one person is unable to come up with a new word, he or she is out. Play until no one else can think of any new words. This activity should draw out several pet peeves as well as inconsequential offenses and more serious observations about people your group members don't particularly like. With all of these synonyms in mind (and perhaps written on the board as well), have someone read Matthew 5:43-45. Follow with a condensed summary of Steps 4 and 5, focusing on the Bible passages, Repro Resource 6, and relevant applications as you have time.

Step 2

The essence of this session can be summed up with three words: "Love your enemies." Of course, you could meet for hours discussing various specific considerations of what this means. But since you don't have hours, simply have someone read Matthew 5:43-45. Then, for the rest of the session, ask questions to help group members understand what Jesus was saying. Begin with *who* your kids consider as enemies and *what* those people did that still causes friction in the relationships. (Group members need not answer these aloud, but should have specific people and offenses in mind.) Move on to *why* and *how* we should love our enemies. Draw relevant material from the session—especially the need to pray for enemies. In discussion, each group member should refer to "the people I've thought about," rather than using actual names. Finally, save enough time to help group members think about *when* and *where* they plan to initiate the reconciliation process.

Step 3

Explain to your group members that God loves the city and wants to redeem it. Then share and discuss two essential Scripture verses concerning God's love:

• I Corinthians 13:8—Love (agape) never fails (falters, becomes invalid, or comes to an end).
• I John 4:18—There is no fear (phobia) in love.

Then explain that agape (God's love) is not a mushy, bleeding-heart love, but a confrontational, tough, rugged, unaffected-by-anything love. In short, real agape is fearless because God is all-powerful. Next, have your group members come up with a list of "Ten Things People in the City Fear Most." Then ask how your group members can use love (tough, fearless agape) as a practical force to confront each item on the list. Finally, choose one or two ideas that your group will actually use in confronting in love as social action.

Step 4

To present anger and sin on a social level, ask: **What things about the city make you angry?** List group members' responses on the board as they are named. Then say: **It's good that you're angry; after all, anger is an indication of injustice. But what I want to know is what you're going to do with your anger.** List these responses in two columns: "Anger That Curses" and "Anger That Blesses." Afterward, challenge each teen to begin to transfer his or her just anger into some form of action that can bless the person or situation with which he or she is angry.

Step 2

Some young teens are just beginning to hold serious grudges. Some haven't formed real enemies yet. Be sensitive to this as you discuss the information in this step. Instead of going through Repro Resource 5 as written, list on the board some of the main characters from *The Wizard of Oz*— Dorothy, the Wicked Witch, Scarecrow, Tin Man, Cowardly Lion, the Wizard, etc. Then ask: **When it comes to conflict situations, which of these characters do you act most like, and why?** Some kids may say they're like the Scarecrow, not thinking before they speak. Others may say they run away from conflict like the Cowardly Lion. Still others may say they're mean like the Wicked Witch of the West.

Step 4

If your kids don't enjoy roleplays, try another approach. Bring in a large supply of modeling clay. Give some to each person. As you describe the following situations, group members should shape their clay in a way that describes how they feel.
• **A kid at school makes fun of the way you look as you're undressing in the locker room. This person continues to make fun of you every day.**
• **You tell a secret to a friend, who promises not to tell anyone. The next day, your "secret" is all around school.**
• **There's a really weird kid at school wthat no one likes. He knows he's obnoxious and uses that to his advantage. He goes out of his way to embarrass you in front of your friends. You don't treat him as badly as some kids do, so he's starting to hang around you more. He sits with you at lunch every day. He calls you at home. He's starting to tell people that you're his best friend.**

Afterward, have group members mold their clay into a symbol for loving enemies. Then talk about each case again, describing what it would mean to love that person.

Step 2

Briefly review the parable of the Good Samaritan (Luke 10:30-37). Discuss the difference between an enemy and a neighbor. Have kids paraphrase the parable in a modern setting, using these characters: a person with AIDS, a professing homosexual, a gang member, someone who is pro-abortion, a drug addict, a person in prison, a guy who gets a girl pregnant and claims no responsibility. Ask: **How, specifically, can a Christian show love to these people as the Samaritan showed love to someone who was supposed to be his enemy?**

Step 4

Read aloud the following poem:
O Lord,
Remember not only the men and women of goodwill,
But also those of ill will.
But do not remember the suffering they have inflicted on us,
Remember the fruits we brought thanks to this suffering,
Our comradeship, our loyalty, our humility,
The courage, the generosity,
The greatness of heart which has grown out of all this.
And when they come to judgement Let all the fruits that we have borne Be their forgiveness.
AMEN AMEN AMEN
(From *Lord of the Journey* by Roger Pooley and Philip Seddon, eds. [London: Collins, 1986].)

Have kids guess the circumstances surrounding the writing of these words. Then explain that they were found on a piece of wrapping paper next to the body of a dead child when Allied troops liberated the Ravensbruck concentration camp from the Nazis in 1945. Over 92,000 people died there. Discuss the kind of love for enemies expressed in the poem and whether it's humanly possible to show this kind of love. Point out that such love is supernatural. Only God can bring it about.

Date Used:

Approx.
Time

Step 1: People You Love to Hate _____
o Extra Action
o Small Group
o Extra Fun
o Short Meeting Time
Things needed:

Step 2: Combat Styles _____
o Little Bible Background
o Fellowship & Worship
o Mostly Guys
o Media
o Short Meeting Time
o Combined Junior High/High School
o Extra Challenge
Things needed:

Step 3: Love in Enemy Territory _____
o Extra Action
o Large Group
o Heard It All Before
o Little Bible Background
o Urban
Things needed:

Step 4: What Love Looks Like _____
o Small Group
o Large Group
o Heard It All Before
o Mostly Girls
o Mostly Guys
o Urban
o Combined Junior High/High School
o Extra Challenge
Things needed:

Step 5: Prayer Conquers All _____
o Fellowship & Worship
o Mostly Girls
o Extra Fun
o Media
Things needed:

Why Should I Give Money Away?

YOUR GOALS FOR THIS SESSION:

Choose one or more

☐ To help kids examine what the Bible says about money and possessions.

☐ To help kids understand the dangers of greed and the importance of giving.

☐ To help kids choose ways they will share their resources.

☐ Other _____

Your Bible Base:

Mark 10:17-27
II Thessalonians 3:10, 11
I Timothy 6:10
I John 3:17

Found Money

(Needed: Play money, a real dollar bill, envelopes)

Before the session, you'll need to place several pieces of play money in envelopes and hide the envelopes around the room in places that will be difficult to find. You'll also need to hide a real dollar bill in one envelope. When group members arrive, explain to them what you've done and give them a few minutes to find the money.

After the money is found, congratulate the person who found the real dollar bill. Then ask the rest of the group members how they feel toward the person who found the real dollar. Note any feelings of jealousy or greed.

Ask: **Did you feel that way toward _____** (the one who found the real money) **before you arrived?** (Probably not.)

How many of you came to the meeting expecting to get a dollar bill? (Probably no one did.)

If you weren't expecting to get any money today, then why are you upset with _____? (They were presented with the opportunity to find money with little effort on their own, and they're sorry they missed it.)

Explain: **Today we're going to talk about money, greed, and giving, and how they're all related.**

Teen Talk

(Needed: Copies of Repro Resource 7, pencils)

Distribute copies of "The Teen on the Street" (Repro Resource 7) and pencils. Say: **Here are some comments that typical high school kids might make about giving.**

Ask six volunteers to read aloud the six parts on the sheet. Encourage the volunteers to use accents or strange voices. (To make your volunteers more comfortable, you might want to demonstrate a strange voice for them. You could hold your nose while you talk, use a high or low voice, or speak with an accent.)

Explain: **As these parts are read, put a check mark by the comments that resemble any thoughts you've ever had about giving.**

Afterward, take a poll to see which of the attitudes is most common among your group members. You'll want to make a note of group members' responses on your sheet because these characters will be mentioned in subsequent steps, and you'll want to know which attitudes to spend more time on.

Hooked on Money

(Needed: Bibles, chalkboard and chalk or newsprint and marker)

Have your group members turn in their Bibles to Mark 10:17-28. Ask for three volunteers to read the speaking parts of these characters:
- Jesus (vss. 18, 19, 21, 23, 24, 25, 27)
- wealthy man (vss. 17, 20)
- disciples (vss. 26, 28).

Write the references on the board so the readers can find them more easily. A narrator (you or one of your group members) should read all the words between the speaking parts.

Afterward, say: **Today's tough teaching is the command Jesus gave the wealthy man: "Go, sell everything you have and give to the poor, and you will have treasure in heaven." Many Christians wonder what Jesus meant by this.**

What do you think He meant? Was He commanding all Christians to give everything away, or just this wealthy man? If no one mentions its, point out that this is the only situation recorded in the Bible in which Jesus made this command. However, verses 28-31 show that the disciples voluntarily did so and were commended for it and promised blessing because of it.

Why do you think Jesus asked the wealthy man to give away everything? (Riches were very important to the man—perhaps even more important than Jesus.)

Jesus told the man he would have "treasure in heaven" if

he gave everything to the poor. **Is giving to the poor a "price" we can pay to be saved? If not, how do you explain Jesus' words?** (No. Jesus paid the only price necessary for our salvation on the cross. Salvation is a gift of God, not the result of our works [Ephesians 2:8, 9]. However, Jesus does talk about "counting the cost." Becoming a Christian does cost us something; it costs us ourselves. Jesus said that anyone who is not willing to "take his cross and follow me is not worthy of me. Whoever finds his life will lose it, and whoever loses his life for my sake will find it" [Matthew 10:38, 39]. Jesus identified the cross for the rich young ruler—it was giving up his possessions.)

It's interesting that when Jesus said it's hard for the rich to enter the kingdom of heaven, His disciples were shocked. "Who then can be saved?" they asked. Point out that in those days, being rich was considered a sign of God's blessing. **So Jesus is saying the exact opposite of what the disciples would have expected.**

What do you think Jesus meant when He said, "With man this [a rich man being saved] is impossible, but not with God; all things are possible with God"? (Jesus' words indicate that salvation is impossible for anyone by human means because it is a gift of God's grace. Perhaps it's harder for rich people because they're used to depending upon themselves. If they think their wealth means that they've pleased God, they might not think that they're sinners in need of God's grace.)

Do you think it's a sin to be rich? (No. For example, Joseph of Arimathea, who owned the tomb in which Jesus was buried, was a rich man [Matthew 27:57-59]. But according to Mark 10:23, it is difficult for a rich man to enter the kingdom of heaven.)

Have someone read aloud I Timothy 6:10. Then ask: **If being rich isn't a sin, what's wrong with money?** (Nothing's wrong with money per se, but the love of money is at the root of all kinds of evil. The problem is greed.)

How is greed at the root of all kinds of evil in the world? Have you seen examples of this? (Greed is behind all kinds of corruption in society. Some people will do anything to get or stay rich. They will exploit others, lie, cheat, steal, or even kill.)

Explain that this kind of greed can happen to anyone, even us. Say: **To love money is to become hooked on it. We begin to think we need all the things it buys. Then, before we know it, we don't own our possessions—they own us.**

How can our possessions own us? (We spend a lot of time buying, repairing, and taking care of our possessions. We discard them before they're worn out to buy bigger and better versions of them. We work so hard to make enough money to buy them that we neglect ourselves, our relationship with God, and our relationships with other people.)

Teen Talk Revisited

(Needed: Bibles, Repro Resource 7)

Refer back to Repro Resource 7. Have group members look again at the characters' comments. Ask: **Is being hooked on money limited to those who have it?** (No, Waldo the Worker is a good example of someone who could get hooked on money because his family doesn't have it. If you don't have it, it's easy to think having money would solve a lot of problems.)

If Waldo the Worker continues his present level of fascination with money, how do you think it will affect the following areas of his life:

• **His family?** (Waldo may choose not to have a family. But if he does have a family, he probably wouldn't spend any more time with them than he does his teenage friends.)

• **His friends?** (Any friends he has will probably be from his job because that's all he'll have time for. He could become a lonely person who has only his "toys" [possessions] for company.)

• **His choice of job or his purpose in life?** (He certainly won't have time to focus on what God's purpose in his life could be. He will only think about how much money he can make, not about whether he's doing something necessary and worthwhile.)

• **His spiritual life?** (If he has any interest in spiritual things, it will be smothered by his obsession with making money. God will definitely take second place.)

Do you think Waldo's focus on money would go away if he inherited a million dollars? Why or why not? (Acquiring money doesn't usually decrease the desire for it. For instance, when your grandparents give you money at Christmas, it's wonderful at first. But then, it's not enough to do all the things you'd like to do with it and you wish you had more. If you have a serious case of loving money, it's agonizing because you'll always want more.)

Look at some of the other teens' comments on this sheet. Do any of them agree with Scripture?

Have someone read aloud II Thessalonians 3:10, 11. Point out that in the early church, people took care of one another. There was no government welfare or social security system. The church fulfilled that function. Each member who could work was expected to care for his family's own needs as well as contribute to the community, so that those who could not work would be taken care of. A lazy person would then become a drain on the community. Paul says lazy people should not be given a handout because that would only reinforce their dependence on the community.

Say: **Lorenzo the Logician's comment seems compatible with this verse. But what's wrong with his attitude?** (For one thing, he's assuming that all poor people are lazy, which is not true. And he does not seem compassionate at all.)

Have someone read aloud I John 3:17. Then say: **Lorenzo the Logician needs to read this. Francesca the Fanatic's comments seem to be a blunt version of this. What's wrong with her attitude?** (Francesca cannot blame all the poverty and hunger in the world on Christians. Jesus even said, "The poor you will always have with you" [Matthew 26:11]).

What is I John 3:17 talking about? (This verse is talking about the needs a Christian sees, but does not respond to. It's talking about being insensitive to the needs that are all around you.)

Christians shouldn't be blamed for all the suffering in the world, but sometimes we don't see things because we don't want to see them. What are some of the obstacles that keep Christians from seeing the needs around us?

Write group members' responses on the board as you discuss them. Use the following suggestions to supplement their responses.

(1) We may not be *aware* of the poverty around us because we are so caught up in our own worlds.

(2) We may not *want* to know because we don't want to cut down on the ways we're currently spending money.

(3) We may not know *how* to help, so we'd rather not know about needs that we don't think we can do anything about—it's too depressing.

What's wrong with Penelope the Problem Solver's approach? (While it may seem compassionate and biblical, it's totally unrealistic. She wants to fix everything for people instead of doing what she can to help them help themselves. Her approach is smothering.)

Point out that Jesus met specific needs of needy people, but He left their dignity intact. He healed their blindness, but they had to remake their lives. If you just throw money at people, you haven't helped them for the long term. There's an old saying—if you give a man a fish, you feed him for one day. But if you teach a man how to fish, you feed him for a lifetime.

Look at Talulah the Too-Young-to-Be-a-Giver's comment about teens being too young to give. Does her reason for not giving make sense? (If you wait until you're an adult to start giving, it will actually be more difficult for you because you'll have no "practice." Anyhow, the Bible doesn't differentiate between "teen commands" and "adult commands.")

Why is Owen the Ower's argument not valid? (Teen expenses may be high, but adult expenses are even higher. If you start using Owen's excuse now, you'll probably use it for the rest of your life.)

The Biggest Obstacle of All

(Needed: Copies of Repro Resource 8, pencils)

Refer to the list of obstacles you wrote on the board earlier. Point to Obstacle #1 ("We may not be *aware* of the poverty around us because we are so caught up in our own worlds").

Say: **We may not be aware of poverty and starvation because we avoid it. We avoid it because it's so unpleasant. When a program about starving kids comes on TV, we probably switch the channel.**

Distribute copies of "How Rich Am I?" (Repro Resource 8) and pencils. Give your group members a few minutes to complete the sheet.

Then say: **If your score is 30 or above, you're "rich" by global standards. Most of the world's population do not have any of these things. People in North America earn more money in one year than many people outside North America will earn in a lifetime.**

When Jesus told the wealthy man to sell everything he had and give the money to the poor, He was not saying that this is the ultimate solution to poverty. What did He mean? (Jesus knew that the man's possessions were more important to him than anything else. Jesus was testing the man to be sure he was really serious about obeying what Jesus said.)

Point to Obstacle #2 ("We may not *want* to know because we don't want to cut down on the ways we're currently spending money").

Say: **How sad that this so often is our attitude. But I John 3:17 reminds us that we cannot claim to be God's children if we do not have compassion on those in need. Giving to the poor is a mark of a person who has the love of God in him or her. So what can we do?**

Point to Obstacle #3 ("We may not know *how* to help, so we'd rather not know about needs that we don't think we can do anything about—it's too depressing").

Say: **Let's not shut our eyes and ears to the needs around**

us because we don't know how to help. What are some things we can do to meet real needs?

Conduct a brief brainstorming session to come up with practical suggestions for meeting real needs. You might want to concentrate on three areas: awareness, prayer, and involvement.

Don't underrate awareness. It's the first step. Some people cut themselves off geographically from certain areas or neighborhoods. Find out what's going on in your community. Are there homeless? If so, is there anybody trying to do something about it? You could appoint several kids to form a task force to find out what's going on in your community—both in terms of need and in terms of what kinds of efforts are already in place to meet those needs. They can keep the rest of the group updated for prayer and, ultimately, for involvement.

Kids can get involved in anything from volunteering at a homeless shelter or a soup kitchen to starting an after-school program of recreation and tutoring to keep kids off the streets. Your group could also sponsor a child overseas through a relief organization, or participate in a summer service project locally or cross-culturally. As you brainstorm, try to steer group members away from *only* giving money. There's nothing wrong with giving money, but personal involvement is far better.

Have someone reread I John 3:17. Then say: **God doesn't command us to give to the poor so we'll feel guilty and grouchy. He does it because it teaches us to be like Him—giving, while expecting nothing in return.**

Close the session in prayer, asking God to show your group members how much He loves the poor and how He wants us to reflect that love.

The ▶ Teen on the Street

Francesca the Fanatic

"How can Christians say they love others, and then let them starve? Tell me that!"

Waldo the Worker

"I have to admit it—I work hard because I like to have money. My family doesn't have much, but I like to buy nice clothes and stereo equipment. So while other kids play sports or hang out with friends, I work to make money. How can I be hurting anyone?"

Talulah the Too-Young-to-Be-a-Giver

"I think it's crazy to ask teenagers to give money to the church or to help the poor. We have plenty of time to do that later."

Lorenzo the Logician

"I don't understand why I should give money to help people who sit around and won't work."

Penelope the Problem Solver

"When I see people begging on the street, I'm totally messed up. I just wish I could take them home with me, buy them a house, and fix their lives."

Owen the Ower

"People all around the world have problems, but so do I. Why do I have to help the world? Storing up treasures in heaven is fine, but my car insurance is sky high here on earth!"

How Rich Am I?

Give yourself five points for each item that's true for you.

_____ The main meal at your house consists of more than rice and beans.

_____ Your parents/guardians pay for your health care needs.

_____ A school is available for you to attend, free of charge.

_____ Your grandparents have access to social security and/or pension plans.

_____ No one at your house goes to bed severely hungry.

_____ Your family is able to buy or charge something—a TV, a refrigerator—
when they need it or within a few months after they need it.

_____ Your family lives in an apartment or house bigger than a tool shed.

_____ Your family owns a car.

_____ Your family owns two cars.

_____ Your family owns one car for every person in the family who drives.

_____ Your apartment or house has two bathrooms.

_____ Your apartment or house has three bathrooms.

_____ Your house has indoor plumbing.

_____ You have a telephone in your house.

_____ TOTAL

Step 2

When you "take a poll" to see which of the attitudes on Repro Resource 7 are most common among your group members, ham it up a bit. Let your six volunteers who represent the characters stand in front of the room. One at a time, have them repeat their comments. After each one, use "applause meter" techniques (clapping, cheers, whistling, etc.) to have students indicate their agreement with each statement. They may applaud for more than one person, but should vary the degree of enthusiasm (volume) depending on which comments they *most* agree with. After each of the six people has been evaluated, you might want to eliminate the ones who received little support and try again with only the top two or three.

Step 5

To wrap up this session on giving, you might want to let your group members practice among themselves before trying to apply what they've learned on a larger scale. Challenge them to give a gift to everyone else in the group. The gifts may be things they have in their pockets or purses, things they find on the grounds (such as dandelions—stealing should be discouraged), or things they make from available materials. They may give actual gifts or symbolic ones (a rock to symbolize strength, etc.). They may give gifts of service, represented by handmade coupons. This may not be a simple activity, but it can be a lot of fun. And it's also a good exercise to help kids start seeing that they can be creative in their approach to giving.

Step 3

With a small group, by the time you include three or four people in an activity, you may as well include everyone. So in addition to the people already involved in the speaking parts for the story of the rich young ruler, add a reporter and let everyone else become observers who witness the event. After the actual reading, the reporter should "recap" what was said (as is done after political speeches) and then try to get crowd response by interviewing the witnesses. He or she might also want to interview the rich guy to discover his feelings, his future plans, and so forth. The disciples could be questioned to shed light on why Jesus appeared so demanding in this situation. As a result of these interviews, the students will probably cover many of the questions that are included in the session after the reading. And even if they don't, you could "prompt" the reporter and deal with much of the information in the context of the skit rather than a traditional question-and-answer follow-up.

Step 5

As you discuss how to apply what you've learned, you may need to put more effort into a "pep talk" for a small group. In many cases, a group with only a few people may also have few resources, a low budget, and limited opportunities to do the things *they* want to do—much less shell out a lot of cash for others. Group members may already have a strong awareness of need, and perhaps be active in prayer, yet may be too discouraged to be actively involved in addressing the problems. Gear applications specifically for your small group—nothing grandiose or unrealistic. Perhaps kids could start by committing to help their own church. While kids may not have a lot of extra money, they usually have free time on their hands that could be "given" to the church to mow yards, paint, repair, clean, and so forth. After they see that they can make a difference there, perhaps they will be more willing to think bigger.

Step 2

Introduce the topic of giving by asking several volunteers to create worthy "causes" and make speeches to get others to give to those causes. (Volunteers may use real organizations or create ones of their own that they think would cause other people to give—even if they are "scams" to put money in their own pockets.) The rest of the group will represent the elite people of society, gathered to hear the "pitches" of all the worthwhile organizations seeking funds. Each person has $1,000 to spend—if he or she can be persuaded to part with it. Give your volunteers a few minutes to prepare. As each person makes his or her pitch, write his or her name and "cause" across the top of the board. When all of the pitches have been given, have each person determine how to spend his or her money. Group members may give it all to one person, split it among two or more, or keep it if he or she didn't think any of the causes were worthwhile. This exercise may reveal some truths about the world of fund-raising. Does most of the money go to the best cause or to the person who was most entertaining? Was it difficult to get people to part with their money? Was it hard for anyone to ask for donations?

Step 4

You might consider dealing with your "Teen on the Street" concept in a talk-show setting. Your six characters can be a panel on the stage, you can be the host, and the rest of your group can be the audience. After each person makes his or her initial statement, have panel members remain in character as audience members ask questions and make comments. Most of the information in Step 4 can be covered in this format, and may get your kids more involved. (With six people to keep up with, however, you might want to provide large nameplates to put in front of your volunteers for easy identification.)

Step 1

After you do the money hunt, but before you announce the topic of the session, give everyone an imaginary $100 and ask how he or she would spend it. Group members may break the money down however they want to—spending it all in one shot or breaking it down into a lot of little purchases—but they should be as specific as possible. As everyone explains how he or she would spend the money, listen for any emphasis on giving, tithing, charities, and so forth. (Some of your kids may figure out where you're headed and say what you want to hear. If so, you could ask other group members to confirm if what your "giving" people have said sounds correct.) If few people give consideration to allotting a portion of their "windfalls" to the church or to needy people, you should have their attention as you go into the rest of the session.

Step 3

As you discuss of the rich young ruler (a story many of your group members may be familiar with), reward correct answers with quarters or dimes. Don't explain. Just keep asking questions and see if the interest level increases. If so, later you can point out that the actions of group members confirm the teaching of the Bible text. Whenever a choice must be made between spiritual commitment and desire for material possessions, spiritual things too often become secondary. You might want to add one more question: **Based on what you learned from the story of the rich young ruler, how many of you are willing to give what you received from answering questions to the church, wait for treasures in heaven, and follow me through the rest of this session?** Anyone who chooses to return his or her money to the church should be congratulated, and then challenged to maintain that same giving attitude when more than dimes or quarters are involved.

Step 3

If this is one of the first times many of your group members hear the story of the rich young man and Jesus, it may not make sense in light of all they have heard about Jesus so far. But before you even begin to explain, let kids express their opinions in a debate. Divide into two teams to debate this topic: "Jesus had no right to ask the young guy to give up *everything* before he could follow Him." It may be tempting to jump in and try to clarify certain points, but simply make note of such things as kids debate among themselves. Later, depending on how the debate goes, you may need to spend a while explaining that this is one of the harder Bible stories to fully understand. After you go through the rest of Step 3, check to see if everyone seems to understand. If not, take more time for questions before moving on.

Step 5

The entire concept of giving might be new to some of your group members. So rather than closing by providing various alternatives for giving more faithfully, you might instead want to explain the importance of giving. For example, many kids new to Christianity may not have any idea where the money comes from to run a church. Emphasize that the pastor's salary, the building, the hymn books, the electricity, and everything else is paid for from the giving of congregation members. In addition, the church may be supporting missionaries in various parts of the world or providing ministries to help the people in the community. Sometimes we tend to deal with the topic of giving as merely a personal discipline and obligation. But if kids see *where* the money goes, giving can become an exciting incentive. So don't rush into the "how you can give" section before you deal with what can result from regular giving.

Step 3

After discussing the story of the rich young man, have kids do "personal possessions inventories." Ask each person to create a list of top ten possessions, in order of personal value. Then ask each person to draw a line at the point in which he or she would have difficulty parting with an item if requested to do so as part of his or her commitment to Jesus. Explain that the young man in the Bible story apparently wasn't a bad guy; but money was tops on his list, and he just wasn't able to let go of it to follow Jesus. If kids confess to owning things they aren't quite ready to give up, don't put a lot of pressure on them at this point. Perhaps they will never be expected to give up what they've listed, but they *will* be expected to put their relationship with Jesus above any piece of personal property. If they are having trouble doing so, they should pray about the matter, asking God to become so close to them that they will desire a relationship with Him above anything else they might be offered.

Step 5

The session provides a number of possible actions that can be taken to get involved with the needs of other people. But you might want to take a different approach. Yes, your kids can give money. Yes, personal involvement is even better. Yet the best possibility for ongoing results is to help group members discover what their skills are and get them involved in some area where they feel comfortable and competent. Ask each person to list his or her strengths, interests, talents, and abilities. Then, as a group, try to figure out good ways to "give" those skills away for the good of others. For example, people with good singing voices can get involved in nursing-home ministries. Those with mechanical skills can help repair church lawn mowers or vehicles. Those who enjoy little kids might be able to teach or assist with nurseries or Sunday school classes. Try to show ways in which almost any talent can be "given" to others.

MOSTLY GIRLS

Step 2
As you distribute copies of "The Teen on the Street" (Repro Resource 7), ask your group members to make the following changes before the parts are read: Change Waldo to Wanda, Lorenzo to Lorena, and Owen to Owena. While the volunteers are preparing to read, give them the opportunity to add a few sentences to what their characters say.

Step 3
Have your volunteers read the speaking parts of the people in Mark 10:17-28. Then ask three other volunteers to read the same passage. Have one person read the part of Jesus; have another read the part of a wealthy businesswoman rather than the wealthy man; and have the third the part of one of the women who followed Jesus, instead of the disciples. After the story is read with these changes, ask: **If the people involved were women, would this change your response to this story? Why or why not?**

MOSTLY GUYS

Step 3
Don't overlook the opportunities involved with having a Bible text centered on a young *man*. Your guys may not relate to being rich, but they still have youth and masculinity in common with the character. Point out that Jesus loved this guy (Matthew 10:21). Then ask: **Why did Jesus let this young man walk away? Couldn't He have tried to convince him a little harder?** Explain that Jesus always gives us choices as to whether or not we follow Him. **But what if we don't make the right decisions concerning our relationships with Him on our own? Based on other people you've seen who put money before anything else, what can happen?** The whole Yuppie movement has shown that wealth in itself is not fulfilling. Guys can acquire the best cars, homes, and clothes that money can buy, and still feel intense dissatisfaction. Nothing can fill a person's inner, spiritual hunger except Jesus.

Step 5
Theoretically, most people will agree that giving is important; yet, in real life, many of us find other uses for our money. To help your guys think through their actual commitment to giving, provide them with a number of activities to consider. Have them suppose they've agreed to give a portion of anything they make to the church during the next year. However, during the year, a number of opportunities come along. They won't have enough money to do the activity *and* give anything to the church. Which activities might persuade them to skip their regular giving for a while? Choose activities you know your group members would especially enjoy, which might include:
• a spring break beach trip
• a white-water-rafting trip
• a ski weekend in the Rockies
• buying leather school jackets
• a date at the coolest (most expensive) place in town.

EXTRA FUN

Step 1
At one end of the room, place a big pile of loose change with plenty of quarters, dimes, nickels, and pennies. At the other end, form relay teams. Explain that you will announce an amount of money and a number of coins. Teams should provide the exact amount using the number of coins you specify. The rules are as follows:
• The change must come from the pile across the room.
• Only one person at a time can go to the pile of change. That person must return to the team before the next person can go.
• Team members can only transport one coin at a time.
• Any extra change must be returned to the pile (one coin at a time) before you will accept the total.
     You might ask for the following:
     • Change for a dollar, using four coins. (Four quarters.)
     • Change for a dollar, using six coins. (Three quarters, two dimes, one nickel.)
     • Change for a dollar, using 17 coins. (Two quarters, three dimes, two nickels, ten pennies.)
     Teams may have difficulty organizing to get the exact number of coins needed. Listen for any arguments or accusations. You can refer back to such comments and show that if we're ready to fight over nickels and dimes, then larger amounts of money might lead to *real* conflict if we're not careful.

Step 2
Have your group members play a drawing game using Pictionary rules (no talking, no words or symbols, etc.). Divide into teams. Have a player from each team come look at a word you will show him or her. The person should then return to the team and, at your signal, draw something that will help team members guess the word. The first team to do so gets a point. Use words connected with the session's topic: *money, greed, giving, possessions, selfishness, sharing, riches.*

Step 3

The movie *Indecent Proposal* got a lot of publicity for the ethical question it raised: Would it be worth a million dollars to a young couple for the wife to spend one night with a stranger? If any group members have seen this movie, ask them to report on it. Then ask: **What do you think is the minimum dollar amount most people would ask for to commit each of the following sins:**
• **adultery?**
• **premarital sex?**
• **murder?**
• **shoplifting?**
• **lust?**

   Indecent Proposal also dealt with the guilt and second-guessing involved after the decision had been made. Ask group members to consider whether they think the rich young man ever regretted *his* decision. If so, have them write a plot synopsis for *Rich Young Ruler 2: The Sequel* to describe what they think might have happened to this guy after he turned down Jesus' invitation to follow Him.

Step 4

Have group members form a couple of "camera crews." Give each crew a camcorder. Instruct the crews to do actual teen-on-the-street interviews. (This could be done prior to discussing the content of Step 4 or as a follow-up activity sometime after the session.) First, crews should create a list of questions they could ask to get to the heart of other people's attitudes toward money. Then they should go to some public place, explain what they're doing, and get people's permission to ask a few questions and record the answers. (You might want to provide some adult supervision for this exercise, but the adults should remain in the background as the kids do the interviewing and taping.) Then return to watch the tapes and see how *real* teens feel about money, possessions, giving, and so forth.

Step 1

Repro Resource 7 is used quite heavily in the session as written, so one option to shorten the meeting is to work around it. You can begin with Step 1, eliminate Step 2, and move to Step 3 without any break in continuity. Also eliminate Step 4 and pick up again in Step 5 where you hand out copies of Repro Resource 8. Skip the references to Obstacles #1, #2, and #3 (which were listed in Step 4), but otherwise follow the text of Step 5 as you wrap up the session.

Step 2

Another option is to focus almost entirely on Repro Resource 7. In this case, you can deal primarily with Steps 2 and 4. However, almost all of the Bible content is in Step 3, so you should summarize the most important points as you move from Step 2 to Step 4. Also, Step 4 ends somewhat abruptly, so close with some of the best suggestions for practical application at the end of Step 5.

Step 2

With an urban group, you might want to supplement the statements on Repro Reource 7 with the following typical urban excuses for not giving:
Rashan the Poverty Stricken—"My family is poor and on welfare; we hardly know where our next month's rent is coming from. What I have I cannot give."
Lae-Li the Minority—"Because I am a minority in a racist country that doesn't want me, I can give only to those who are of my cultural group."
Julio the Neglected—"I have some money; but no one ever gave me anything when I was in need, so why should I give to others?"
Feather the Old Soul—"This city has existed for nearly two hundred years, and poverty hasn't gone anywhere except up. No amount of money can make a change. I'd rather hold onto my funds."

   Refer back to each of these characters in Step 4.

Step 3

Have your group members consider how a conversation might have gone between Jesus and each of the following people:
• a prostitute
• a gang leader
• a drug dealer
• an alcoholic
• an abusive parent
• a superstar athlete
• a straight-A student.

   Ask: **How might the conversation have been similar to or different from the one between Jesus and the rich young man?**

Step 2

A group with a lot of young teens might not find Repro Resource 7 as effective as older groups. Junior highers may not yet have strong opinions (if they've formed opinions at all) about social concerns, giving, and so forth. Many still expect their parents to take care of such things. Yet they also frequently have an intense craving for more and better possessions—the best athletic shoes, bicycles, clothes, and so forth. Your time may be better spent helping them identify and express their attitudes and helping them see the "big picture" concerning the use of their monetary resources. Show them the importance of starting *now* to set aside a portion of what they have for the church and/or the support of those who are less fortunate. Help them see that if they don't begin now, it will never become any easier.

Step 5

As you discuss practical applications of what has been discussed, you'll probably need to get more specific with junior highers. The session text has some good ideas, but young teens usually want to see for themselves what needs to be done. As you deal with awareness, prayer, and involvement, take kids through each stage. For awareness, walk around the church grounds and see where improvements could be made if more money were available. Or drive around the sections of town where your group members don't usually go and look at the needs of the poorer people in the community. For prayer, challenge the kids to begin to pray for others on a regular basis (which may be quite different from the usual "personal request" prayers of many young people). And finally, when you get to involvement, try to come up with some suggestions (to begin with) that are short-term, and that your students can do on their own. Explain that you will expect accountability, providing an opportunity in the future for each person to describe the results of any actions he or she chooses to take.

Step 3

To help your group members get a better perspective on the story of the rich young man, have them read the parables of the hidden treasure and the pearl (Matthew 13:44-46). Ask: **How do these parables relate to the story of Jesus and the young man?** (The men in the parables who discovered the treasure and the pearl were able to recognize the value of what they had found. They knew it was a "real deal" to trade everything they had to acquire their new-found treasure. But the rich young man in real life failed to see that following Jesus was a far better treasure than the pile of money he had at home.) Also have group members discuss some things they can do to ensure they don't make the same mistake the young man made.

Step 5

Sometimes we are unable to give our time or resources to others because we are unaware of their needs. People may not like to admit that they are "needy" in any way. So without referring to *needs*, have each student make a list of "Things I Wish I Had" and "Things I Could Use Help With." Explain that these should be serious concerns—not fantasy cars or dream vacations. When they finish, collect the sheets and make a master list. (If you wish, you can keep the names, but make the master list anonymous.) Then in the weeks to come, students should see if they can help with the concerns of other group members in some way—by sharing possessions, helping with difficult homework assignments, or whatever. It may be difficult for your group members to get serious about helping others if they are ignoring each others' needs.

Date Used: _____

Approx.
Time

Step 1: Found Money _____
o Heard It All Before
o Extra Fun
o Short Meeting Time
Things needed:

Step 2: Teen Talk _____
o Extra Action
o Large Group
o Mostly Girls
o Extra Fun
o Short Meeting Time
o Urban
o Combined Junior High/High School
Things needed:

Step 3: Hooked on Money _____
o Small Group
o Heard It All Before
o Little Bible Background
o Fellowship & Worship
o Mostly Girls
o Mostly Guys
o Media
o Urban
o Extra Challenge
Things needed:

**Step 4: Teen Talk
Revisited** _____
o Large Group
o Media
Things needed:

**Step 5: The Biggest
Obstacle of All** _____
o Extra Action
o Small Group
o Little Bible Background
o Fellowship & Worship
o Mostly Guys
o Combined Junior High/High School
o Extra Challenge
Things needed:

Custom Curriculum Critique

Please take a moment to fill out this evaluation form, rip it out, fold it, tape it, and send it back to us. This will help us continue to customize products for you. Thanks!

1. Overall, please give this *Custom Curriculum* course (*Too Tough?*) a grade in terms of how well it worked for you. (A=excellent; B=above average; C=average; D=below average; F=failure) Circle one.

   A   B   C   D   F

2. Now assign a grade to each part of this curriculum that you used.

a. Upfront article	A	B	C	D	F	Didn't use
b. Publicity/Clip art	A	B	C	D	F	Didn't use
c. Repro Resource Sheets	A	B	C	D	F	Didn't use
d. Session 1	A	B	C	D	F	Didn't use
e. Session 2	A	B	C	D	F	Didn't use
f. Session 3	A	B	C	D	F	Didn't use
g. Session 4	A	B	C	D	F	Didn't use
h. Session 5	A	B	C	D	F	Didn't use

3. How helpful were the options?
   - ❑ Very helpful   ❑ Not too helpful
   - ❑ Somewhat helpful   ❑ Not at all helpful

4. Rate the amount of options:
   - ❑ Too many
   - ❑ About the right amount
   - ❑ Too few

5. Tell us how often you used each type of option (4=Always; 3=Sometimes; 2=Seldom; 1=Never)

	4	3	2	1
Extra Action	❑	❑	❑	❑
Combined Jr. High/High School	❑	❑	❑	❑
Urban	❑	❑	❑	❑
Small Group	❑	❑	❑	❑
Large Group	❑	❑	❑	❑
Extra Fun	❑	❑	❑	❑
Heard It All Before	❑	❑	❑	❑
Little Bible Background	❑	❑	❑	❑
Short Meeting Time	❑	❑	❑	❑
Fellowship and Worship	❑	❑	❑	❑
Mostly Guys	❑	❑	❑	❑
Mostly Girls	❑	❑	❑	❑
Media	❑	❑	❑	❑
Extra Challenge (High School only)	❑	❑	❑	❑
Sixth Grade (Jr. High only)	❑	❑	❑	❑

---

6. What did you like best about this course?

7. What suggestions do you have for improving *Custom Curriculum*?

8. Other topics you'd like to see covered in this series:

9. Are you?
   ❑ Full time paid youthworker
   ❑ Part time paid youthworker
   ❑ Volunteer youthworker

10. When did you use *Custom Curriculum*?
    ❑ Sunday School   ❑ Small Group
    ❑ Youth Group   ❑ Retreat
    ❑ Other _____

---

11. What grades did you use it with? _____

12. How many kids used the curriculum in an average week? _____

13. What's the approximate attendance of your entire Sunday school program (Nursery through Adult)? _____

14. If you would like information on other *Custom Curriculum* courses, or other youth products from David C. Cook, please fill out the following:

   Name: _____
   Church Name: _____
   Address: _____
   _____

   Phone: (_____) _____

   Thank you!